Chri Unwrapped

Visions of Christmas Reality

Clement SkyGazer

I heard about this book on Public Radio (Harbor Springs) When the author was interviewed in Dec. '97.

Rhodes & Easton
Traverse City, Michigan

Copyright © 1997 by Clement SkyGazer
Skyrunner Publications, Inc., Leland, Michigan
Edited by Shelley Watkins

Published by RHODES & EASTON
121 E. Front Street, 4th Floor, Traverse City, Michigan 49684

Publisher's Cataloging-in-Publication Data
SkyGazer, Clement
    Christmas unwrapped: visions of christmas reality / Clement
    SkyGazer – Traverse City, Mich.: Rhodes & Easton, 1997
            p.   ill.   cm.
            ISBN 1-890394-02-5
        1. Christmas—Personal narratives. 2. Gift books.   I. Title.
    GT4985 .S59   1997   97-68268
    394.266'3 dc—21   CIP

PROJECT COORDINATION BY JENKINS GROUP, INC.

00 99 98   ❖   5 4 3 2 1

Printed in the United States of America

DEDICATED

 M ostly to the stars of my life, Holly my best friend, only lover, and forever wife... and Logan Nicholas, Christy Mara, and Noah Christopher, our beloved three.

To Mom, the pre editor.

And to the "Audience:" Pat, Donna, Lena, Fr. Charlie, Sue, Tito & Rhonda, Walt & Dale, Fr. Bob, Pete & Flo, Mary & Bob, Dona & Danielle, Joe & Kathy, Kim & Family, Mark & Mary Helen, Pfleger & Tierney, Cynthia & Rick, Curt & Sheroma, Mike & Sue, Burg, J.C. & Dulce, Ed & Jan, Mary & Kurt, Fr. D., Chandler, Kathleen, Dr. Michael, Diane & Marilyn, Sam & Diane, Bubba, Don, Laura, Jill & Dan, Joyce,

Dedicated

Terry & Barb, Bob & Colleen, Lee & Molly, Aunt Dotty, Donna, George & Patti, Gary, John & Julie, John, Aunt Delma, Cathy & Fred, Bob & Char, Dennis & Julie, Mike & Connie, Eilleen & Ryan, Len & Mary, Jeff & Nancy, Loren & Barbara, Chris & Julie, Hank, Jan, Brett, Barbara, Annette, Audrey, Geralyn, Ray, Matthew, Carol, Gloria, Loren, Jo & Chip, and Mom & Dad & Trish.

Also to the many employees of Northwest Airlines who watched me write a lot of this as I rode their planes and who encouraged me to publish what I wrote.

You are responsible. It was you who kept saying year after year...

You should get it published.

Special thanks to Shelley, my managing editor, who understands my voice.

Because of Pfleger

CONTENTS

FOREWORD

All human actions have consequences which continue on through time. Parents do things which affect their children, like their parents before them influenced them, and so on all the way back to the first parents. This is a thread that connects us all.

The recounting of these actions has been the business of storytellers, poets, and bards throughout the ages. Today the news is the method of telling stories. But the news storytelling has devolved into mostly a recounting of acts which hurt. In my day we called it committing sin.

Your stories, children, need some help.

So I asked the Master of us all if I could do some notice-able nudging to get some good news, some good tellings, back into your lives.

I know this may look like a violation of "the rules" be-cause I have made the Great Leap, and supposedly the chasm blocks the return. It is not that those who have gone on to what is are not among you. We are simply complete in our Master's plan, and so can see everything. You can not, or you would be here. Except on rare occasions when one of you reaches and reaches, with not themselves at heart, but only reaches for the sake of What reaches back, we can not show you what we see. But we can nudge.

The truth is, you wouldn't believe the nudging that goes on from this Side. It is sad the many many times our nudg-ing gets ignored, or tossed into the category of "that's im-possible, I can't believe that!".

Yet we keep doing it. We are relentless. Some day, when you are whole, you will understand.

I sat in on this entire book. Clement, who runs the sky and wrote the words, often sensed me. I am always flattered when written about, although it still mystifies me why I ended up with so much attention. There are many (and Someone) who deserve more.

I think Clement blends well what I was with what I am.

I think, too, that he has blown some dust off the thread of life, that tiny immensely powerful strand that winds its way back through each and every life, all the way to the Spinner of the thread. You've covered it with dust, with so much of what is not, stories of what is wrong.

Thank goodness it is so strong, this thread of life. I see it in all his stories, and if you read them, you might grasp and feel this thread. Hold it tightly in your hands. Learn again what it is.You will read about things that are right, very very ancient, and deeper in reality than even he suspects.

St. Nick

PREFACE

*T*his book is a series of letters written over a ten-year period to a group of close friends and family. It is about the beliefs, traditions, values, and realities of the living Christmas. I want to awaken or re-awaken your belief in Christmas, that point in time and place where God's magic, things normally unseen by earthly eyes, becomes real and nature and the stuff of heaven dance together.

Please do not confuse the reality to which I testify in the letters that make up this book with the supposed reality that is reported on televisions, in newspapers, in magazines, or by people who say, "Did you hear..."

Preface

I ask for no agreement with my beliefs. I only hope something of what I have recorded, even a tiny little piece, strikes a chord in you, or fans a spark, and your eyes, the ones that are the windows to your soul, open, and ...

You will see!

And believe!

Even just a tiny little bit!

Letter One
TRACKS

*W*hen I first started to write Christmas letters, I often composed them as I raced through the sky at somewhere between thirty thousand and forty thousand feet. Apart from a spectacular view of planet Earth and the awesome miracle of Creation, it was a quiet, peaceful, solitary place to write.

This letter started over Greenland. I was in the company of people inside the plane, but outside?

There must be angels out there. What else could survive at thirty-eight thousand feet outside of an airplane? Deep dark blue frozen air—filled with angels?

Christmas Unwrapped

What do you think keeps these planes up?!
This one is about Christmas of 1991.....

❋ ❋ ❋

The Christmas Season in our house begins the day after Thanksgiving when, still stuffed with fixings of the Day of the Turkey, I roll out of bed about seven in the morning.

Yawn. Stretch. Bones crack. Snap. Up. Ooooooh! Feeling my morning's first awakened moments, I pad unevenly in bare feet into the kitchen.

First things first. Coffee. Cowboy coffee. Those of you who do not know what cowboy coffee is... well, if your spoon doesn't stand up in the middle by itself when you are through brewing, it isn't cowboy.

Silently, I start to make sandwiches. I lay out rows of white squishy bread bought specially for this moment. I test the bread for mushiness with my fingertips, probing and pushing.

Having approved the mushiness, I pull the roaster pan from the refrigerator and take off the aluminum foil. The turkey still looks good. I slice the turkey with a serrated knife until I think I have enough. I coat the bread, each piece, with mayonnaise, licking excess from the sides of my fingers. I always get mayonnaise on my fingers as I scrape around the inside of the jar. There's a rhythm to that sound of a metal knife scraping and tapping the inside of a glass mayo jar.

I add the turkey slices, lettuce, and a dash each of salt and pepper to the one side of mayo-coated bread. I wrap the finished sandwiches in waxed paper, seal them in plastic bags, and put them with drinks and other snacks into the cooler. These and other necessary items for the task of the day, the great Christmas Tree hunt, I load into the car.

I pause.

I think.

"I wonder if there will be any unusual Magic this year?"

I wait.

The Silence of All That Is answers nothing back. Oh, well, time to gather the mission participants.

I hoot, holler, bark—more than a few times. Got to wake up those sleeping. Wake up the kids. Want to see if there are any dead around who might want to get up, too.

Into the van and the four-wheel-drive pickup pour three generations. Armed with Christmas tapes and blankets and Christmas books, we head for the hills.

Our mission is to seek out, hunt down, and kill, four big, old, and beautiful Christmas Trees. It is upon their death that they cease to be a pine or spruce and become what all trees desire to become, if only for a moment, a Christmas Tree. Scotch Pine, Blue Spruce, Douglas Fir. We spare no species.

The place we go to is pine tree heaven. Thousands of acres. Loaded to the max with evergreens. There are rolling, gentle, northern hills. Hills that pour forth from where we stand like round waves, covered with pine and snow. Sometimes we can see the pines and the snow roll with the waves. Usually the sky is a brilliant deep blue, that rich color Michigan keeps to herself. Sometimes snow falls gently. This year, there are both, Michigan blue and snow, intermittently.

The trip is as always, warm, snowy, comfy, Christmassy, full of laughter, cheer, and burr-laden dogs. The quest for the perfect tree. Adult and child cooperative decision making at its finest.

No! Not that one!

Then… Yes! This one!

The annual slaughter of trees of needles takes place. We offer our apologies to the environmentalists.

A day or so later the next step of Christmas takes place.

Outside lights—my job. Grandpa, or the Poppa as we call him, helps a little. The kids less. They do love darting in and out and oogling and ogling as strand after strand is tested and placed in its proper spot. We weave them first throughout the roping that drapes the entrance way to this house of Christmas. Then we staple them onto the top rail of the split rail fence that separates the front walk from the yard. Across it they go, perfectly spaced, tips pointed to heaven. Then they go into the trees; three dogwoods, three Japanese maples, three pines. Front and back, we coat the nine top to bottom. More lights are purchased. Leaving them up half of the year has the usual effect of rusting out a good number of them. No one who sees this display doubts the presence of Christmas celebration in this house. Chevy Chase as Griswold in *National Lampoon's Christmas Vacation* would be jealous.

Days pass. With the Christmas tree in the garage and

the lights up, the children careen further and further out of control. They do not count the days. They count the minutes. Sprinkled in during the time it takes to get from the taking of the tree to the Eve of Christmas Itself are Advent wreath making, nightly appropriate readings like *How the Grinch Stole Christmas, Rudolph the Red-nosed Reindeer, Santa's Gift,* and *The Polar Express,* and the massive interior decorating.

This alteration of the decor of our home happens exclusively and in its impeccably tasteful manner by the Queen of the house and her cohorts. Except that is, for the raising of the tree and the putting on of its lights.

That is my job, again. Lights take about three and one half hours. Getting a light every square inch is partly to blame. At least this year I do not have to fight the sharp needles of the Blue Spruce. Somehow I managed to talk the Queen into a Douglas Fir, whose needles are soft, a living velvet of needles. I am spoiled now; henceforth, only Douglas Fir will do.

Lights finished, the Queen and her cohorts swarm the evolving masterpiece like bees, buzzing in and out, pollinating every branch with the ornaments and decorations, bought and handmade, maybe one from Christmas present, mostly from Christmases long past.

Christmas Eve. Certainly this night, as in every Eve of Christmas Itself, the Angels, or if you prefer C.S. Lewis's description, the Elidils, bring their wonder down to earth. There has to be more magic on this day from Above than any other. Preparation maybe? What is that I smell in the air...?

Children to whom I teach about God in religious education classes I often ask...

> "Who was born in a stable, in an animal feed
> station, of very poor parents? Who received

little if any formal education, at least as we would know it, throughout His life? Who never had a steady job after leaving His earth father's carpentry business? Who never led a company, never led a country, never led an army? Who was certainly considered a rebel by the leaders, religious and otherwise, of His time? These leaders plotted to have Him killed and eventually did so. Yet, most of the world marks its time by His birth."

Is there a better time for magic than this momentous occasion....?

Finally, all preparations are in order. The house is full of Christmas.... From the little white votive candles burning merrily in small glass holders everywhere.

To pine boughs spread gracefully from staircase to chandelier, to fireplace mantle, to Nativity Scene.

23

From the glowing, glittering Christmas Tree that seems to fill a third of the room.

To smells of balsam-scented incense.

To harpsichord Christmas music.

To children dressed in Christmas green and red.

To the glowing Queen, my wife.

The hour approaches four in the afternoon of the Eve. Time for church. The children's service. It's not quite the midnight celebration, but it's always awe inspiring.

We head for church. We walk. The day is already growing dark at four in the afternoon. Overcast. Gray. Dark gray. Cold. Colder than brisk. Bare ground. There isn't any snow. Every other year we have lived in Michigan there was snow for Christmas—except one. Unusual and disappointing.

The church is packed. All the Christmas Christians are making their annual pilgrimage. I am glad to see them come to honor Him if only this once a year. Always are they welcome by Him. Kids are everywhere, and that is an understatement. Out of twenty-five hundred families belonging to this church, every one with children is there.

The air is not quite one of hush. Anticipation floods the building's atmosphere, suffocating all else. Christmas carols begin to penetrate the thickness with the feeling of what is to come. First a piano sounds the season like a harpsichord, then the organ. The hand bell choirs join in. People begin singing. The volume increases, rising to a crescendo. It is steady and full, but not overpowering, lasting for thirty minutes before the start of the service.

The kids start this process sitting still, but craning their necks, as if searching every corner of the inside of that place of worship, looking for signs. Eventually they squirm out of their seats. Scurrying now, they move about. They run up to look at the Baby Jesus in the Nativity Scene. They crawl under pews. Then it's stretching to see, standing on the benches, looking for signs. Oh, well, it is their service.

We sing again. Sing praise! Sing carols! Bask in the presence of the Angels, who with so many children present, lose control of themselves and bathe the place in Glory. You know the kind. Glory. Angel-led Glory. Heaven's Glory.

> *Glory to God in the Highest! And on Earth Peace*
> *To Those on Whom His Favor Rests. For Today*
> *Is Born To Them…"* Luke 2:14.

Hallelujah! You can sense, almost feel the brush of Their wings!

The Spirit carries this collection of a thousand people— big, small, old, young, middle-aged, ancient—throughout the service. Warm. It is so warm. People smile and embrace. Hands are shaken. Hugs happen over and over. "Merry Christmas!" "Merry Christmas!" resounds again and again.

And again.

Christmas Unwrapped

Be there now. Feel it. Squeeze the hand of a friend or loved one. Feel their surrounding arms as they hug the hug of Christmas. If only it could be this way beyond this Day......

With the last chorus of "Joy to the World" fading into the heavens above, lifted by the voices of all, eventually drowned out by a rendition of Handel's _Messiah_ from the church organist, we head for home.

Lo! Behold! As we walk through the church doors and out into the now night, the first miracle of Christmas—

Snow!

Magic it is, rain turned magic by the breath of Winter, falling from above. White Christmas! It is thick, too! Definitely sticking. Homeward we go. Skipping. Slipping. Shouting. Shrimp and clams and "smoked things" await us. Plus one present per child. The snow thickens. I did not know it then, but more miracles were coming.

The Queen and the twin wonders, our younger son, Noah,

and daughter, Mara, head into the house. Logan Nicholas, a true child of Christmas born two days before, and I are in charge of the luminaries. The whole street lights them. Every year. All the way up and down the road. Like a village from Christmas past. The walkway and the roadway lit by candle.

Picture this in your mind. The light of candles, illuminating the snow-filled air, all the way down a small town's snowy Christmas Eve street.

Inside it is Christmas Eve, too. Good food. Good drink. Good music. A great roaring fire. Peacefully quiet. All of us gaze out the window at the softly falling magic; thick, white lace, settling onto everything, surrounding even the white twinkle lights on the split rail fence, turning them into softly glowing blobs of Christmas white. We settle in with one another, cozying up against.

Then it is bedtime. Time for the sleep that the little

ones think will never come. Out come Santa's treats—cookies, milk, carrots for the reindeer. We allow the fire to die.

The big discussion. "What time are we allowed to come down?" Coming down too early might result in catching The Man in the act. Stay awake too late—same thing.

"Why don't we set an alarm and when you hear its ring, it's safe!"

This talk with our little people about a timely entry was prompted by last year's experience.

After finally getting things arranged by 2:00 A.M. the Queen and I awoke to a face in ours at 3:00 A.M. whispering hoarsely, "Dad! Dad! He's been here! He's been here!"

I responded from a total stupor. I mean, come on, be serious folks. Wouldn't you if you had been assembling toys for hours, working nervously as you go, thinking some little soul might come down and "catch" you?

"Are you sure?" I mumbled. "Go back and check."

Pitter patter feet sounds, the kind that come from a child wearing one of those sleepers that zip up in the front and have feet with plastic soles, faded off and away, down the hall.

And then quickly back.

"Yup! He's been here!" The total elation-filled response.

This year we were shooting for six A.M. The Queen and I finish the preparations. It is amazing the nervous sensations that twittered through us as we hoped our four- and six-year olds did not come down and catch us in the act.

As we settle in for a "long winter's nap" with Christmas music softly lulling us, the Queen jolts me.

"Did you hear that!?"

"Hear what?"

It sounded like...

I had heard what she heard. It sounded kind of bellish, kind of tinklish, kind of wooshing, definitely whirling, and magical. Maybe even Super Natural.

"Must be Santa!"

We both laugh in conspiratorial mirth, smiling at each other, knowing it could not be.

And yet... as I turned over to sleep, oh so peacefully, a bit of wonder, like traces of star dust, drifted in my mind.

Awoke at five. Could not sleep. Way too excited. Got up. Checked out everything to make sure it was as we left it at one A.M. Munched down the Santa treat. Was it all there?

Left some traces for effect. Scooted some ashes out of the fireplace and onto the hearth.

Or were they already there?

Put on the cowboy—coffee, that is. Crept up the stairs and slipped three presents under the small tree the kids kept upstairs without waking them. More magic. Sat down in the living room wing chair with a cup of cowboy and amidst all the Glory of the Day, lit the Tree, and waited.

The alarm sounded at six with a blare. Up I went, shutting it off after I entered the room saying, "Merry Christmas! You can come down any time now!"

But, they all turned in their beds and kept on sleeping.

The Queen and I ended up with an hour and a half to ourselves. Never do we get such a luxury. Christmas morning and just the two of us—the starters of this immediate family.

Our trio of wonder eventually came down. For two hours they recreated, or maybe I should include us big kids too, we recreated, nuclear expressiveness at its most powerful. The Bomb. Detonation. Everywhere.

The children hauled their booty up to their rooms to play more intently with it and perhaps get a better look than they could in all the confusion. The Queen and I sat immersed in the Glow. Wrappings everywhere. Contented smiles. Just sitting softly and quietly and contentedly.

We did good, and we knew it.

Then we hear the scream.

The Scream.

Classic scream.

Right off the couch it shoots us, as if a bolt of pure electricity had burst up from the couch cushion and galvanized our spines.

Terror?! Panic?! Pain?! Excitement?!

Couldn't be sure.

"Dad! Mom! Come quick! Come see this! Come see! Come quick!"

Over and over this high-pitched chant poured down the steps at us.

Up we ran. Up the stairs, in a heart beat we were there. Called by Something beyond the voices of our children.

There, standing by the window, the one that looks out over the garage roof, the window next to the fireplace chimney, stand our three children. They are white as angels from

33

the reflection off the snow on the roof of the winter early-morning sun. The look on each face is absolute.

Absolute wonder.

Before I tell you what they are looking at I want to mention one thing. Our kids are good at recognizing tracks. They know the difference between the rabbit, the squirrel, the deer, the fox, the raccoon.

"Look Dad! Tracks!"

I approach the window.

There, in perfect order on the garage roof, following a southwest to northeast path, right up to the chimney, were the delicate tracks of deer!

Letter Two
THE SAINT

I *think this one started hitting the page over Nebraska. There was a classical music selection pounding away inside my head. You know, like when you listen with headphones. Snow covered the patchworked landscape over six miles below. This time we cruised at forty-one thousand feet.*

Above the earth.

Having met with a bit of success with last year's letter, I'd been thinking for several months what to put in this one. Thousands of thoughts drifted for months in and out. People who know me don't find the thousand thoughts very strange. When you have an atten-

tion span like I do, often like that of a six-year old, you can get a thousand thoughts a minute.

But all those thoughts had to wait.

Something happened that I can not explain. I am sure I'll never be able to explain it. I can only tell you what happened, just before Christmas of 1992.

❋   ❋   ❋

It happened on November 1, the day some call the feast of all saints. The feast of all of us, I hope, someday. A few days back but seems like another lifetime now. Perhaps it was.

November dawned gray and blustery. Halloween, the sugar event of the year, was over. We were glad to be done with it. The day of "Trick or Treat" had been sunny, but cool. The temp hovered in the forties but, with a decidedly heavy East wind that picked up as the day went on, I sensed we were in for some weather. Our cooler-than-normal summer seemed to be speeding the transition into an earlier-than-normal winter.

As Holly took down the spectral decorations, the kids and I went out to play. Down cascaded the leaves, ending their lives like huge colored snow flakes. Trees shed themselves of their autumn finery almost at once. It became too gray, too dark gray, too cold. Ferocious. Heavy. Heavy weather. At times, as I stood watching the kids pile the leaves into a huge mound, diving in, and smothering themselves to avoid the cold, I felt my eyes closing. The howl of the North Wind engulfed me closing out all else. I felt myself drifting off, sucked up into the great northernness, the Up-North state of mind, almost into a deadly sleep. Then it began to snow...

Deep Magic at work, I suppose. But then I believe in magic, the stuff of God that one can only explain as miracles.

We packed it in early. Strange. The kids didn't complain. They wanted in. Very strange.

The polar bear trio wanting in? The three who swim in water at forty-five degrees with the air temp at fifty. Who play in snow until they become snow people themselves. This is the same group that dragged me into the lake in early October.

Never mind that the air temperature was fifty-eight, or the only thing about the water temp that I was sure about was that it was above freezing. I knew that because there wasn't any ice yet on the surface.

"But Dad, it's sunny!" was the rationale I fell for.

Into the house we went. Hauled in some wood. Last year's. This year's hasn't been delivered yet. Started the fire. Got it roaring quickly. Years of enjoying a pyro-mentality does have its practical benefits. Turned up the heat. Made soup for dinner and some garlic bread even though the threat of vampires was over for another year. Had hot chocolate, of course with marshmallows. Gathered some books after dinner and sat down in front of the fire to read.

Blankets, sleeping bags, books, us, and the fire. Wish the glow of that scene could be described in words... golden memory doesn't seem to suffice.

And still it snowed... So unusual...So early...

After reading out loud for almost an hour, Noah, one of the twin wonder children, stumbled across a book from Christmas, *The Polar Express*. Whether you have kids or not, if you haven't read it, you should. See which of you can still hear the magic of the bell.

We read the book even though it wasn't yet the Christmas season and then settled into talking about the stuff of Christmas. We reminisced about the lights, the Nativity, the trees, the cookies, the toys, the greens all around, the pine.

The smell of pine....

We remembered the scents, the joy, the kindness that comes from people even if at no other time of year.

The children fell asleep. Literally. This has never happened to our kids except in a car or in a bed. They just do not dose off. Yet there they were, fast asleep. Peace. I don't ever recall seeing such peace. Individually, or as a group. Their faces described peace like I...

I can't explain, there are no words.

And the slight smiles. Pleasant thoughts must be in their heads, I mused. Sugar plums maybe? They were glowing. Ridiculous. Kids don't "really" glow. Just the light and flicker from the fire, I suppose.

Had to carry them all up the steps, for the first time in a long time. The act struck a bittersweet note in the center of my heart. Too soon they would be too big. As their strength increases, mine wanes.

Gently, I tucked them in. I asked the Blessing of the

Master on them as I do every night. I touched their faces. I left their rooms gazing at their sleeping forms thinking of Wendy Lady from the movie, *Hook*, intoning,

"Light of night protect my sleeping babes, keep them safe throughout the night..."

The wind howled relentlessly. I shuddered as I walked down the steps.

Reaching the bottom of the steps I anticipated cozying into the living room with my best friend and only lover and a roaring fire. And still it snowed...

Settling back into the wing chair with the ottoman under my feet, I began to read. Intense warmth came over me. Sweetly suffocating me. Peace. Softness. Through eye half open I took note of Holly, my wife and the Queen of this house, lying across the couch, already asleep with a book face down on her chest. Her pleasant everyness was my last thought before...

41

The banging on the door startled me out of my peaceful reverie. I looked at the clock. Midnight.

Exactly.

My watch. Same thing.

The banging continued. "Who can that be?" I thought. "At this hour!" Someone must be in trouble. I got up. Staggered. Still groggy, I looked at Hol. Fast asleep. Weird. That woman wouldn't sleep through a pin dropping, and yet, so peaceful she looked. I went to wake her and say something like, "Babe! Babe! Did you hear that?!"

Before I could open my mouth the banging on the door stopped me as if to say, "Don't wake her. Come let me in instead."

So I went to the door. Fear gripped me. The banging hadn't repeated. Was "it" still there? Had "it" gone away? With the world the way it is today, with the violence, the crazies, the murders, maybe I shouldn't open it.

I peered through the peephole and saw nothing but swirling gray black, frozen fog at midnight. I opened the main wooden door. It creaked and scratched, the sound of wood scraping across the metal door stop. Only the storm-glass-covered screen door stood between me and... the outside.

My fear intensified banishing any vestiges of warmth and peace and encapsulating my soul in ice. This fear was both a physical terror and the "Fear of God" type. All I saw beyond the glass storm door was the swirling black fog—ice fog. I was looking into total unknown, the outer darkness or blackness. A blackened whiteout, a new twist of intensity. It was scary. Very scary. I hesitated. I knew I did not want to open that storm door. Then something seemed to take over my hand and guide it to the latch.

Down I pushed it. The die was cast.

The storm door blew and crashed open. Snow came swirling in, sparkling with a light of its own, in miniature blinding colors. The Northern Lights splashed on the floor around me in bits and pieces of multi-colored glitter.

All of a sudden He was there. A man with the most brilliantly jolly face I have ever seen. Old for sure but....ageless? His smile dropped my fear to nothingness.

"King Clement!" He exclaimed. "So very good to see you again!"

The "King Clement" greeting startled me. I stood there in shock, my mouth agape. Then I began to take in what I was beginning to think was an apparition—if thinking was what I was doing.

He looked familiar.

This was either a wildly wonderful dream, or I was beginning to understand in a very real sense the concept of nervous breakdown.

The "apparition" wore below that merry and very bearded face, a white top, open at the neck, like a long underwear flannel shirt, black pants with a wide belt, shiny I think, and a pair of combat-like boots. I think. The boots were shiny, too. I think. I think. I think. I think.

I know. I can see it as clearly as if He was in front of me right now. I just keep struggling with the belief. There was no doubt about the shine of that belt and those boots. Maybe they weren't really combat-ish. So familiar, but so unplaceable.

"Well, aren't you going to ask me in?" He laughed with a boom.

A boom that reverberated inside my head. A voice I heard inside my head. I was losing it.

"You are not losing it," He said. "Please, may I come in?" His face mellowed in concern.

The voice was gentler now. I shook my head. It cleared. I also noted that I was shaking my head. Really shaking. Maybe this wasn't a dream. I dug my fingernails into my palm. It hurt. I wasn't dreaming. My head was still shaking. Side to side.

I said vaguely, remembering my manners, "Ummm... of course. Please do."

In He came, touching my arm as he entered the front foyer. With that simple amiable contact a thrill ran through me, the sensation an explosion of tinkling sounds like teeny, not tiny, bells. There was smell too, a sweetness like that of pure spring. Spring flower smell completely permeated the room. Stick a flower right up under your nose and inhale and you'll get an understanding of about one thousandth of the smell I smelled. And yet, it was not overpowering.

It was as light, or lighter, than air.

The air itself took on a color. I guess it was a color. Gold. It glowed. Never saw air glow before. Must have been the light from that fire again. I do build great fires.

He walked into the living room. Looked around, smiling as he took in all that was there, pausing in his gaze at the pictures and the statues. Then He finished His journey across the room and sat down in the wing chair next to the fire.

He tipped His head at Holly, smiled, and said, "Queen Holly is as lovely as ever. You are well to be with her."

My heart and soul sang at this praise. I knew this was truth staring me in the face and yet still, no words came, my mouth still agape. I still see every detail, as if they seared into my consciousness and subconscious like a branding iron on a baby calf's buttocks......sssssssss! See the smoke?

He looked from Holly to me, "You remain a stubborn man, I see." My quizzical look encouraged Him to continue. "Here I am sitting before you, and you refuse to acknowledge, to believe."

He laughed and when He laughed He shook. This startled me again. So familiar, yet I was sure I'd never seen this man before.

"Ha! You don't recognize me!"

Honestly, I didn't, I thought. I didn't quite feel I should either. There wasn't that guilt associated with seeing a face from long ago and not being able to place the name. We've all been there. Seeing the person. They know your name. They say hello as if you are old friends seeing each other for the first time in ages, and you can't remember their name. So you say "hi" like you really know them while guilt racks you and your memory balks. It wasn't like that. I just couldn't place Him.

He laughed again. "I thought I knew you better," He said. "And I do know you very well. And you come so highly recommended, too, by some dear friends of yours and mine with whom I recently have had the great pleasure to become reacquainted. You know them. Charles and Helen. Bob and Dorothy. Cletus. Tony. Catherine. Thelma. Norb. Rosy. Johnny. Laurien. Jake. Ethel. Herb. Most recently, of course, there is dear sweet Eleanor. And then there are Clement and Catherine." As the names Clement and Catherine came from His lips a shocking revelation blasted into my brain. He was reciting the litany of those I pray for every Sunday at church under the category...

"Welcome into Your Arms those who have left us, especially..."

He laughed again, and oh, how He shook. Yes, like a bowl full of jelly...

NO! NO WAY! I have lost it!

"You have not lost it my good soul friend," He said. "'Tis I."

His eyes twinkled like the Star Itself. His head tilted slightly to the left. A smile so slight it was barely there settled onto His face. He became silent and looked at me. Looked into me. Right into me. Through my eyes, the windows of my soul, and into my heart and touched them—my heart and my soul. Those windows opened like a floodgate, pouring forth tears of the purest Joy I have ever felt. My vision blurred but only for a second. When it cleared, and I looked again into His Eyes of Twinkle I saw there too, the tears coming out, coursing down those robust cheeks, and disappearing into that flowing river of white hair that covered from his face to his belly button.

I knew that He was Real.

"Thank you," He said. "For never losing your belief in me. You are halfway through your thirty-eighth trip around Brother Sun. Almost all people that have come as far as you have forgotten me, or worse, stopped believing. Most stop before they turn ten."

"Why me? Why did you come to me?" The words I uttered escaped from my lungs through my lips like the tiny buzz of a bug, or at best, the voice of a little boy.

"Because you are among the eldest of my still earth-bound

believers, because of those who recommend you, and because I need your help," He said.

"Need my help?" I asked incredulously, my voice gaining little confidence. Kind of like a school child on his first day of school, among strangers, in a strange room, in a strange building.

"Tell people I am Real. Tell people that I exist. Tell them that I become most powerful when I work through them. Because the Sons of Adam and the Daughters of Eve, as our good friend C.S.Lewis describes you, are so numerous, the best and **only way I can touch them is through them.** (Excepting those rare occasions of evidence, like when my deer left paw prints on your roof.) So, they must touch each other. Parents to children. Brother to sister. Friend to friend. And often even stranger to stranger. Tell everyone you know. Tell the world, if you can, that I am Real. I am as Real as you or any Son of Adam or Daughter of Eve. I am the Spirit of Giving. Remember, there was a day when I was a Son of Adam Myself here on this planet."

"I am Real and I Live!"

The words "I Live" shot to the center of every cell in my body, to the innermost molecules and atoms, jolting them. Electricity. Every one of my cells became electrified.

Then it stirred—the electricity. It began to rise. Leaving my body. Into the already golden air of the living room. It became visible as it left me, like billions of very tiny stars all twinkling in a stardust cloud. A miniature Milky Way, only more full of stars. The star cloud hung suspended in front of me. It brightened to a brilliance so intense, like a super nova, I was conscious of nothing else. I was blinded.

Suddenly, it came at me. Struck down, entering me like a heat-seeking missile, right to my heart. Burning, searing, it pierced through my heart muscle, stopping the beat. I blacked out.

I don't know how much later it was when I awoke. The cheery Man was still sitting by the fire. He gazed into it as if in deep contentment. He turned and looked at me.

"I didn't know if you could be the one when I came. You have shown that you still have the "Stuff". It is in You. You can tell the Truth. You can be the Truth."

"I also came, King Clement, because you are in trouble. The last time your children asked you to take them canoeing you said no. Your excuse was false. You told your children one thing, your reason was another. You chose not to take them across the surface of Sister Water one more time because it was too much of a "hassle". You deprived your children. This was one of the times lately when your Spirit has weakened. I came to give you fresh strength."

"Remember, King Clement, although the presence of the dark one—evil—is here, in the end it will be gone, vanquished. There simply will be no room for it. After all, evil is only choosing not God. In the meantime each will have to live with the ultimate God-given gift—free choice. Each will have to choose between the demon of evil and the choice of good—God."

"My good Brother Giles, the dear friend of Francis of Assisi, Francis who brought us the Nativity scene to our celebration of Christmas, probably said it best with:

> *If you have these three things you cannot be evil.*
> *First, if for God's sake, you bear all tribulation*
> *that comes your way.*
> *Second, if you humble yourself in everything you*
> *do and receive.*
> *Thirdly, believe faithfully in all those things that*
> *cannot always be seen with earthly eyes."*

I looked at the Man. Truly I was in the presence of Wonder.

I mustered up the courage for a question.

"Why do You keep calling me King Clement and why do You call Holly, Queen Holly?" I asked. I looked over at Hol. Still asleep in deep peace on the couch. Like Sleeping Beauty, or an Angel at rest. I looked back at the Man.

"No, she will not awake." He said. "This is between you and Me. It is for you to decide whether this will be between you and the world. She will sleep the best sleep of her life as will your children. It is a sleep made from the stuff of the land of fairy tales, the place between sleep and awake. As I passed through that place on my way here, I froze some of the air and turned it into the finest dust. I sprinkled the hearts of your wife and your children. They are in a land of deep Peace and Joy now. They will remember none of this. I dare say though, that when they awake, they will be like never before. Newer. Refreshed. Alive. Glad. Daring. As to your title. Does it make you uncomfortable that I call you what you are? You are the King of this place, this house. Your

55

wife is the Queen. It is this way for all parents and all homes and all Sons of Adam and Daughters of Eve who have children. Your home is your castle."

"Tell me about you and the North Pole," I said as if in a dream. In a dream. In a dream. I dug my nails again into the palm of my hand. I wanted to make sure I was awake. He froze. And paled, becoming almost transparent. I jumped from my chair.

"What's wrong?!" I shouted.

He returned to His merry presence in a flash.

"Your belief," He said. "You doubted your awakedness and therefore My real existence. See how fragile belief really is?"

A huge sigh of relief left me as I stopped in my upward motion. I exhaled loudly. Even as I write this I inhale and exhale that same huge sigh.

Feel it. Do it. Inhale. Exhale. Big ones. Expel all that

you are from your lungs. Feel it rush up from the depths of your chest, through your throat, over your tongue, out past and through your lips. Close your eyes. Feel the relief. That's the sigh I had.

"Ahhhhh! The North Pole!" It was His turn to sound dreamy and far away, the sparkling look returned to his eyes.

"The North Pole is the grandest of all places of the land that lies between sleep and awake. It is the most beautiful Christmas scene you have ever imagined. Picture the mountain village wrapped in the Holiday's finest. Pine trees everywhere. Huge Christmas green pine trees, well-spaced allowing each one to grow perfectly. Mountains capped and laced with snow. Their peaks shining in the light of The Star. The Star shines every day. Only the snow storms, which come every week, once a week, at eight P.M. on Sundays, lasting for nine hours, stop Its Light.

"There are plenty of meadows scattered about. The animals love them. They live there. Rabbits, foxes, doves, wolves, of course, lions, bears, giraffes, (they're a special kind that can stand the cold—same for the elephants), and the reindeer. They get along famously. We keep them well fed. The lions and the lambs are particularly fond of each other, almost always sleeping together. Yes, there is that very special little reindeer with the big red nose that glows in the fog."

"The town itself blazes in color and light. Picture a billion twinkle lights. See them now, squint your eyes a little to get the full effect, all the colors of the rainbow, but with no electricity of the man-made kind. Only magic juice! The cells of the walls and roofs of every home and factory are alive with "The Electricity". They glisten. They sparkle. Every room has a real fire. Through the windows you can see the warmth."

"Inside, you can feel it."

"This time of year it is always night or twilight. The

stars twinkle all the time and there is fine music made of tiny bells in sync with the twinkle. The place bustles with activity except each day when we pause and sing the praise of Christmas."

> *Glory to God in the Highest, and Peace to His people on earth, for today is born unto them a Savior..."* Luke 2:14

"Every day we celebrate the reason we and the North Pole are."

"We and the North Pole are the stuff of fairy tales come true. All of us. The fairies, the angels, the elves, Mrs. S. It is a place of perfect wonder, peace, and delight!.........."

With a great big smile and a very jolly laugh He rose. My heart sank. I wanted to be with Him forever and I knew He was leaving. I suspected that this was the only time in my life here on this planet that I would see Him. He moved to the door, pausing when He reached it. Turning to me,

59

He beckoned me over. I got up and went to Him. Stopping in front of Him, I said with tears flowing down my face, "Thank you for coming."

He smiled a smile that I still see. It was Peace. It was Warmth. It was Joy. It was Love.

"Thank you for believing..."

He vanished out into the still swirling snow. I turned back into the living room. The fire was slowing, almost embers, but it still warmed the room and gave off that fire glow. I sat back down in the wing chair and staring into the last of the coals, wondered and....

I woke with a start. It was bright outside. Looked at my watch. Oh, no! Seven thirty! I have an important meeting with the chairman of the board right now! Thirty-five miles away. What happened?!

Holly came dancing into the room. Her face was alive with a look of pure Happy—not happiness—pure Happy.

"Hello, my lover. You were sleeping straight upright and yet you looked so peaceful. I decided you didn't need a meeting with the chairman of the board this morning. I love you! What a great and glorious day!" Off she pranced.

Squeals of delight were coming from upstairs. Sounded like Christmas morn. The night before came back to me. It was yesterday. No, it wasn't yesterday. It was last night. No, it wasn't last night. Wow, what a dream!. What a dream....

I stood up. Stretching and cracking my bones as I did so. Walking over to the window I looked outside. Only patches of snow were here and there. It was windy and sunny, early morning sunny.

I ambled over to the front door. Opened it. Looking out I saw some snow on the porch. I opened the storm door and a waft of spring-like air came pushing into the house. I stopped and smelled it. Like flowers. I'd smelled that smell before... What happened to that disturbing weather of yesterday? My eyes closed as I drank in that air.

Close your eyes. Drink.

Shaking my head I looked down.

There in the snow in front of the door were footprints. Boot-type footprints. About five inches long. They were coming in and going out.

"Honey, have the kids been outside this morning?" Exhilaration at the possibility making my voice hoarse.

"No Babe, they haven't even been downstairs, yet," Hol called out from the kitchen.

I froze.

"Come here! Hol! Come here! Babe! Come here! Holly! Holly!" I was yelling now.

Feeling her steps more than hearing them, she came with, "All right! All right! I'm coming!"

She pulled up next to me. "What?"

"Don't you see them?" Exasperated.

"See what?"

"Those footprints." I was suddenly whispering. Like someone with a great big secret.

"Yeah...I see them. Hmmmmmm....wonder who made them. Weird, huh?"

"Honey!... Honey! .... Honey!.... Are you okay? Clement? Clement! Hey!" She was shaking me.

She waved her hand in front of my face. I pop back from my trance.

"Yes sweetheart. I'm okay. I'm really okay. I'm fine."

She turned and bounced away. Still on happy feet. I closed the door.

So the story is told. Maybe I was in Never Never Land. Come to think of it, I don't remember verbal words ever being used. They all seemed to be inside my head.

No. Even though it may brand me certifiably a lunatic, I must tell you. I believe. I believe it happened. I believe in St. Nick. And I believe in His power in us. Believe, also. Believe with me!

In the movie, *Hook*, there was a part when Captain Hook had Peter Pan down with a knife to his throat and his hook-for-hand ready to strike. At this moment, Peter's son, John, said to Peter, "I believe in you. I believe you are The Pan."

That simple statement gave Peter Pan the strength to stop the descending hook and throw that mean old man, Captain Hook, across the deck.

Be the Pan to your children. Believe in them. They'll believe in you. Miss none of them. Miss none of it.

One more thing.

Be the Claus to everyone you can.

P.S. You know, you really should keep an eye peeled for foot-prints. Especially on your roof and, I guess, at certain magical times of year, your front porch.

Letter Three
A Love Letter

A bit different from my other letters. I wrote this letter to one person, my best friend and only lover, my wife, Holly. She is the woman I love.

This letter was easy to write when I was giving it to Holly with her Christmas present. Now to share it is much more difficult. It is a story of a love effort told in a love letter. It is the story of a man, in love with a woman, who wanted to get her something very special for Christmas. Some things may be unclear to the reader. For example, you may ask what a Demanding Creature is. Well, all parents have at least one. Otherwise they couldn't be parents.

Christmas Unwrapped

And with that tip to explain to you a little about what you will read, I'll simply leave the rest of the interpretation up to you and whatever other Help that just might kiss your mind as you read some very intimate details about Love, its very Self.

Dear Holly,

I've searched for about a month now. Been on quite a number of trips. Gone to places I wouldn't normally go. Walked almost endlessly; here, there, everywhere. Wonder if I'll find Her. You see, it is for Her that I am searching. Found a trace of Her in a card I saw. The card had two faces in two places. One big face, one small face. In both places in both faces. Traces of Her. Yet, I haven't found **Her**.

Looking. Looking. Looking. High. Low. In between. I want to find Her. Buy Her. Then bring Her home to you, my love. You need Her. I do not even know Her name. I am sure though, I'll recognize Her name when I see it. Or hear it. Angelica pops to mind but that is not it. It is not even close.

My concern, of course, is that it is close to the big day, and I may not find Her.

But I believe I will.

The search is tough. Hours. Becoming days. And weeks. And now a month. It occupies my mind all the time. I've trudged. I've sludged through water and wind and slush and snow on ice. The territories I search are sparsely populated. Not sure if more people would make it worse or better. Lots of people tend to jostle. Then there is our mutual feeling about crowds.

Keep looking. On shelves. On walls. Maybe hanging, maybe standing, maybe lying down. Where is She? I saw One the other day, not Her mind you, who was standing on

His head. She has to be out there somewhere in some form. I know it. Don't ask me why I know it—I just know it.

Why do you search so, you ask? And just who is She? My eyebrows raise as I ponder your questions. Why do I search on and on, and who is **She**? I will answer these questions one at a time.

Why the search... It is early morn. Very dark and cold. Mozart or Bach or some other very dead musician begins to play again in my left ear, as they do every morning. I shut them off, for another nine minutes. Most of the time I shut them off again and again. This drives you nuts I'm afraid. Yet, even though it has been going on for years you tolerate it. You, the tolerant one.

I finally wake. Get up. Go shower.

At this time of year in particular it seems the tension begins immediately for you. If you've slept your mind only whirls an instant before you awake. If not, which is often the case, then it continues to whirl, vortex-like, as you take in what surrounds you. Piles of things to do, undone, everywhere, in every room. Disrepair abounds, in different forms in almost every room. You are worn from the piles, the endless string of beads with no knot at either end. Sometimes you let "the sigh" escape.

And then there are the demands.

Those demands. Those needs to fill. Endless needs. From creatures. Beautiful creatures but endless in their cravings for… almost anything. They demand. They are the Demanding Creatures. They're not yet grown. There are three of them. They need. They need. They need. If you stop giving to the Demanding Creatures, their growth stops, is stunted. It is an awesome responsibility of yours to answer their demands. Without fill from you the Demanding Creatures might lose some of their beauty. All of this you think about in one way or another.

Yet, you get up and begin your trudge. The trudge through your day. You never look at it this way, at least not this early. This morning, though, you did, perhaps because the Coming is so close and preparations are still so numerous.

You have been awake for less than a moment, and Tension, that ugly demon, chortles with delight as he enters your soul and begins his work. He has found a good place to work his black magic and so early in the day, too! He calls his friends. Irritation comes first. Followed by Frustration. Self-Pity lallygags, but Anger comes quickly. Thereafter Despair and Panic. These demons love to follow the Tension Demon anywhere. He is adept at finding the cracks in your defenses.

These demons like getting together until they are together. You'd think they'd party. They do, but it's an evil party. They wreck havoc. They fight for your mind's atten-

71

tion as they wrangle in your soul. They slug each other pushing one out of the way so you have to listen to another. At this time of year it seems as if they are at full crescendo by early morning. If not before the Demanding Creatures wake up, then as they do. Then they receive reinforcements— the Whine Demons.

So, my love, I search for Her because you need a Supernatural ally. The Tension Demon and his friends have made you their battleground for too long. It is time for peace, and you will have It. Again I will go and search.

Five days until it is Most Holy. Still, I haven't located Her. The Tension and Stress Demons are shrieking to get at me. They fear that I will find Her today, and if I do, they know that the end is near for them in you. I am anxious. Another demon maybe. Do I have enough time to find Her, to describe Her?

In a sense my search describes Her. Seeking, looking,

trudging, over long periods, through many places, with no find. Yet, deep glowingly inside, knowing She is out there. Driven to seek Her for you.

"What?" you ask. "You seek Her just for me? There must be something in it for you."

There may be, but I seek Her only for you. Because I believe She can turn the tide on those demons. You do not know this. You have never met Her, or anyone like Her.

The search begins again on yet another close morning. Please let me find Her. Please!

Exactly what is She?

There is no exactly about Her. Your first impression may be that of an image on an icon. You may think the Icon is beautiful or wonderful or neat—or you may think it is none of these. I choose this Icon with great care and thought and time.

So already you see a little of Her. She cares, oh, so greatly and She is a thinker of huge proportions. She cares. She thinks. It's taken hours and days and weeks of trudging and sludging and seeking. That tells you a little more. She persists, at times against great odds and formidable enemies.

"How do you know her if you haven't found her?" you ask. I just know—I just believe She Is.

She is wise. Wisdom went into Her choosing. And not my wisdom. Look at Her qualities. Care. Thought. Persistence. Wisdom. Know that She has all these things because of the Great One—Love. **The** Love. It is this and this alone that continues to drive my search for her. Because I love you and because I think of you incessantly. You are in desperate need of an Angel. A real life Angel. And so I will find Her for you.

An Angel. One who speaks with God and works His magic wherever She goes. And it must be a woman—I think! Off to search for Her some more. Dodging the Tension

Demons and the Anxiety Demons and trying to divert them from you as I search. I will not allow them to keep me from my quest to find you...

... an Angel.

Another day passes. It is late in the evening of then yet another. There are only three days left until the Coming. I found Her today. It was late and dark. My shoes got wet. Again. There were times today when I sweated in desperation. Just couldn't find Her. Had looked everywhere. Had two final shops in mind where I was sure that I would find Her but when I got there, they were both closed...until the 26th. My heart sank.

Pure despair.

It was as I left the last place that I noticed the shop across the street. Quite a lot of things were in there. It was an Icon kind of shop. It was here that I found Her. Way off in an east corner. Hidden among thousands, maybe millions, of

other things. Almost facing the wall, so that She was difficult to see.

I wasn't sure at first. I didn't know if it was really Her,
or if She was just something to buy. I had searched for so
long and didn't want to come home empty-handed. How
could I now be unsure after being sure for so long that I
would know Her?

I wandered the store for another half an hour. Finally, I
came back to Her. She was the last one they had. Maybe the
only one—ever. Apparently this image of Her was wrought
by a woman artist in Germany at least five years ago.

I was unsure. I bought Her anyway. Mostly because of
the Holly leaves. She seemed to be spreading them, or maybe
living in them.

Did not feel too good about Her even after making the
decision. Brought Her home. Left Her in the trunk. Went
out with you for a couple of hours. Came home. Worked on

stuff in the basement. Broke some things, had to vacuum. Tired. Creativity gone. Displeased with Her. (How blasphemous that now sounds!)

Thinking of your words, "It didn't work out, huh?"

"You bet it didn't!" I thought.

Then Her name came!

Holly Angel. She is the Holly Angel! She made me smile instantly! Even though She was still in the trunk! (or at least Her Icon was).

She speaks! Like a laughing wind suddenly turned loose. She talks in the language of laughter. Her voice blows through my mind. She says she will hang by you always! She is used to living in Holly plants, Her laughing melody prattles on. Likes the berries! She's been a most Happy Angel ever since she was—which has been, oh, so very, very long. Think of all that Happiness!

Maybe it's because she is closely connected with the coming Christmas. She told me she was at the First One you know!

She likes to live in Holly plants, or bushes, or trees or whatever they are (which means I suppose that when you don't need Her she'll be hanging out in the front yard in what's left of the Holly bushes that are on the other side of the split rail fence. Maybe She'll make them grow again). More interestingly, She has always helped only people named Holly.

Her Magic is truly wonderful. Full of life. Direct from God. No layers in between, touched by Her (and magical) association with a living plant—the Holly bush. This is so hard to describe.

Imagine you are a mouse scampering over the top of fresh-fallen Christmas-Eve, or Christmas-Morning snow until you found a Holly bush. Then you stopped and huddled for a moment up under one of the leaves and just simply smelled the air, the snow, the Holly, the earth. Well, after you'd breathed it all in deeply you would have a tiny little hint of what this magic of Her's is all about. Just a tiny hint, mind you. It is far too vast for you to know much more than just a little about it. Just a hint will do you fine anyway.

You will like Her Holly Eve. Holy Holly loves. She loves life and She will protect yours. She will care and advise and She will keep your demons away. Believe in Her. She is real. Pray with Her. She comes to you this Christmas to be with you forever. One day you will see Her. Perhaps here. Perhaps **There**. It will be. Smile. She is now yours and you are now Hers, to care, to protect.

God be with you my most beautiful love. Merry Christmas!

Peace be with you, Holly, my wife. May Angels everywhere smile on you and us if even only for a microbeat bathing us in His Glory Amen!

Postscript

Two and one half days left until the Coming. You spoke possibly your greatest line,

"In the process of looking for what I couldn't find I lost what I had found!"

Boy, Is Holy Holly going to be good for you. Oh, I'm still laughing!

This morning when I went to get the newspaper with our dog, the humog (half human half dog), Boundre, Holy Holly was outside. She lit the ground with the tiniest of sparkles, like bits of super glitter, as a late-setting moonbeam she recruited for the light force bathed everything around me. Ahhh! It is good! I am hard pressed to give this Angel to you Christmas morning. She is my friend...

No... the truth is, I am looking forward to giving you this Angel. I will miss having Her just to myself, even though it has been for less than a day. She brightens everything.

Makes it all Merry. And totally demoralizes the Tension Demon. I believe it was She who planted the seed of humility, and knowledge, then growth in you this morning as Embarrassment and Pride terrorized you.

It is like being in a dance with Life Itself to know Her. She carries anything you want to Him who grants all. As I finish this on the Eve of our son's birthday and two days before the Eve of His Coming I sit almost empty, though I am alive with **Joy**. Knowing that this Holy Holly Angel will come to you and protect you and care for you and help you clean and quiet your mind. Knowing that She comes only because I searched for Her and asked Her to come. Selfishly wanting in a way if only for a heartbeat to keep her to myself ... but She and I want none of that.

I smile and think of the Love that brought Her and the miracles She will work as She sings and plays and works with you. My words can not describe what I know to be true. That is my Faith I guess. I know It to be true, and I give It to you. Merry Christmas my beautiful woman! If I thought you were beautiful before—the star-laden sparkles of Angel dust that now surround you forever, will dazzle me into a perpetual mental smile of you! Believe! I do!

❋   ❋   ❋

So the letter ends. But not quite the story. Holly was thrilled with the Angel. Beyond tears. Beyond joy. She loved the gift and the New Friend. To this day many trips of the earth around the sun and passings of moon later, the Angel still hangs by Holly's head at night while she is in bed and helps her through her day. But there was something interesting about the icon.

When I purchased the icon I noticed that on the back of it was an inscription. The inscription read, "Holy Angel". As to this inscription I was sure because I picked up and studied the Icon thoroughly several times before wrapping it up for Its Christmas morning delivery.

After the dust had settled Christmas morning, and the Angel was frolicking wildly through the lives of the family, I had a chance to hold again the icon that had taken so much effort to bring into the house. I gazed into the angel face on the icon. Touched its shape. Then I absentmindedly turned it over...

To the back.

To the inscription.

The electric shrill chill that seared my everyness as I read these words still sends shivers down my spine today as I write them.

The inscription that had once read, "Holy Angel", now read "Holly Angel".

Letter Four
Silent Tears

*N*ormally by early December I have the Christmas letter *written and rewritten. But not this year. Perhaps it was the weather. It mostly rained; the temp always hovering about 33. We had snow on the ground for a while but it melted about five days ago.*

Figured I should get this started, or there wouldn't even be a note in your Christmas/Hanukkah cards.

We have moved to a new and wonderful place. Much more country. Smaller town. I call it, where we live, the Inside. As I sit here looking out my window at the Inside I realize that there is magic in all the small, seemingly insignificant snippets of life which add up to something special. Come share some with me now.

❄   ❄   ❄

December 6th, the feast day of the original Santa Claus, St. Nicholas.

Silent laugh.

Thought of Saturday. Tree raising. Took five hours to get the thing up and put the lights on. Had to begin with taking a chain saw to the trunk to shave it down so it would fit into the stand. No joke. Managed to keep all the four-letter words to myself.

After the tree was in place and ablaze I sat back and watched and listened.

The Queen and her cohorts again began the annual swarm around the great fir. Needed a step ladder. Had to use the second-to-the-top step of the ladder to get ornaments near the top. Bits of conversation...

"Don't grow up!" commands the Queen to her cohorts as an ornament pulled from a box brought a flood of memories from Christmases long past.

Then peeks into the future...

With the Queen telling her children how we'll go over to Mara's house, our twin daughter, and she will ask...

"How do you think we decorated our tree this year, Mom?" To....

"Daddy'll come over to put on the lights!"

Christmas past. Christmas present. Christmas future. All at once.

Silent tears.

Broken up by Noah, the twin son, pressing the bottom of the Shuttle Craft Ornament as he pulled it out of the ornament box and the ensuing...

"Shuttle Craft to *Enterprise*. Shuttle Craft to *Enterprise*. Spock here. Happy Holidays! Live long and prosper!" (In Leonard Nemoy's voice, of course.)

Silent Joy!

December 7th

I drove a Christmas Tree five hundred miles today. To the casual observer this would have looked like a red truck heading down the highway with a white spruce strapped to the top, with the trunk of the tree roped to the front and the tip of it hanging over the back, roped to the trailer hitch.

But me, I was there in the branches, hanging on for dear life. And driving.

Whipping her down I-75 at seventy-five to eighty miles an hour (Ooops! My kids might read this), sixty-five to seventy miles an hour. Wind chill must have been fifty below. Snow, salt, sand sprayed my face and my hair and coated the needles of my tree. Had to hose her down when I brought her to my sister's home.

Her? The tree. A gift to my only sister from the forty-fifth. What's the forty-fifth? The parallel. It's where I live. Halfway between the equator and the North Pole. A real Christmas Tree. A five-hundred-mile, eighty-mile-an-hour Christmas Tree. Yup!

December 8th

Some people celebrate this day as the Feast of the Immaculate Conception. Just think. If this Jewish, peasant-like girl, who while unbelievably pure, had no money, no status in life, only a good boy friend whom she deeply desired to marry, hadn't said yes.... for one thing I wouldn't be writing a Christmas note, and there would be no Christmas trees, or presents, or smiles, or songs, or Christmas lights, or Christmas Light....

By the way her "Yes" almost blew her marriage, the only thing she had. Yet, she did it anyway. Love that Trust concept, don't you?!

Killed my fourth one today. Christmas tree that is. Sunny southern Ohio day—forty to fifty degrees. Made the shuttle to Indy and back in about nine hours.

Got back to the land of Sugar (Poppa and Nana's, my parents', home called Sugarbrush) and sensed that well, maybe they might need some help selecting the proper fir to grace their Christmas living room and season.

So we fired up the red truck and off we went to Cedarville. And there I got my fourth.

Had to really take the chain saw to the bottom of this one. Rrrrrrrrrrrrrrrrrrrrrrrrrrrrrrrrrrrrr!

Had to wire it to the wall, too!

December 9th

Drove another five hundred miles today.

To see a Christmas concert, in a very small town, at a very small school. Everyone from this town was there. Must have been three hundred people, or more, in this small-town, high school gym. Kindergartners sang. First graders sang. (Hey look! I recognize two of them!) Second graders sang. Third graders sang. (Look! I recognize another!) Fourth and fifth and sixth, all sang.

All of them.

Interestingly enough there were several colors of kids, who spoke several languages. They sang in at least two languages. They sang of not just Christmas, but of Hanukkah. Mostly though, they sang of Peace. And their wish for It.

Silent Tears.

December 10th

Today I worked for a period and then began to follow the Queen around. We went to small town shops, in search of things to give for Christmas. The toy stores we shopped in were no bigger than some, if not most, of your living rooms.

This Queen I shopped with is really beautiful. I know it embarrasses her when I say that. But when I look through her eyes and into her soul, it awakens in me the truest of Loves. Suddenly I understand, all over again.

...and marvel, as if for the first time, at my unbelievable good fortune!

December 11th

Wrap-up day. If I don't finish this and send it out you won't get it. Not that this means much. You might be better off if you didn't get these spaces from my space. None the less, I've committed, so you will receive.

The light of this day is just starting to come.

The rain has turned to snow.

Which is certainly magical.

My oldest child wrote Santa this year. A real letter. I thought of sharing the whole thing. Then I realized that this was really between him and Santa. I should not betray their relationship.

I will tell you that my oldest told Santa that even though some of his friends did not believe in Him any more, he still did.

He also told him that he loved Him. Silent tears.

Christmas Unwrapped

Christmas.
The Breath of the Planet, The Wind, is now cold.
It blows through the trees, the nerve endings of our home,
Mother Earth.
Shakes them.
Makes them bend and twist and shudder.
The air and the sky are gray.
Bits and pieces of sea-bred magic flutter and dance.
Solitary voyagers of pieces of white.
White magic.
There are no sounds, except for the muffled roar of the
Breath of the planet, the Wind.
Nothing comes.
Into my head.
Into my heart.
Into my Soul.
Except Peace.

Christmas Unwrapped

So I take a bit of this Peace.

I pick It up.

Hold It in my hands.

Clasp It up against my red and black plaid wool shirt.

Close to my heart.

Squeeze It.

Breathe It.

Close my eyes.

Become It.

Offer It.

For all of you.

In this Season.

That remembers.

When It all came together.

In a cave.

To a teenage girl.

And a husband who made his meager living with his hands.

Witnessed solely by shepherds, whose only roof in life
were the Stars.
Announced by Messengers of The Most High!
Turning a simple place
In a simple world
Into an Explosion of
. . . **ALL THAT IS!**
Gloria in Excelsis Deo
And Peace to His People On Earth!
It came in a tiny baby.
That forever changed the world.
Now I offer It again to you.
From the center of my heart.
Peace!
Silent Tears.
Silent Night.
Silent Joy!

❄   ❄   ❄

Somebody is standing outside the window. About thirty feet in front of me. One of the kids? Must be. The light is not yet that good. Can't tell which one. Must be one of the twins. The snow swirls around the figure as it waves to me.

I wave back.

The figure keeps waving.

No wait. The figure is beckoning.

The door slams behind me. I spin around. It's my daughter, Mara.

"Good morning Tumbalina! I Love You! What's Noah doing out there in the woods?"

"Where Dad?"

Mara walks over to my desk, her eyes fixed out my window.

"Noah's in his room playing. With Logan."

She looks at me.

I look at her.

We both turn simultaneously and look out the window.

Into the woods.

At the little person still standing and waving, or beckoning.

"Do you see what I see Mara?"

Big smile.

"Yeah! Looks like a little man."

"What are those funny dark green clothes he's wearing? Why is his hat so pointed? Why is he standing out there? Why is he waving to us?"

(Mara can be the queen of the Where's, Why's, What's.)

"Look, he's moving away. But he keeps turning back to us."

"He's still waving"

"Dad, he's telling us to come out!"

"Well, what are we waiting for? Let's go see what he wants."

I'm beginning to feel a little funny about this. I've had this feeling before. The butterflies in my stomach are starting to flutter with a certain type of wild delight.

We put on our coats. Pull down the hats. Pull on the gloves and head for the door.

To the outside. Of the Inside.

Letter Five
GABRIEL

*D*ecember Second

My best friend and only lover and I began this day with a cup of coffee. It was my making, so the spoon stood in the middle, and the caffeine-induced energy sparked our bloodstreams. I am going to take you all on a walk now, and as I walk, I will jot you a few notes to go with this year's story.

Excuse me while I go put on my L.L. Bean boots and fur-lined leather aviator helmet hat and ski gloves......

I step outside. Hol, the Queen, is still inside, so I decide to go feed the birds. I put seed in the one wood feeder that hangs from a big, not giant, white pine. This tree is about ten feet from the boys' window. Their window is on the second story. I've rigged a pulley system so that I can raise and lower the feeder. This allows it to be right outside their window. It helps in their study of the magic of birds.

A very few flakes of snow are falling. One at a time. Several seconds apart. They're about the size of nickels.

Hol comes out and looks around for me. Spots me. I finish raising the feeder back up and walk over to her.

We head around to the back of the house, trudging through about eight to twelve inches of snow still lying around from the forty we've received so far.

We push up the rise behind our house, where the great white pine sentinels live. It's really a big clay dune that ends up overlooking the great freshwater sea, Lake Michigan.

Deer tracks are everywhere. I look closely. They all still look to be whitetail. No reindeer yet. Some tracks are large. Must be the Prince.

Of the forest you know.

We head up and around, first on the two tracker, then onto the gravel road that runs to Lake Street. It is icy. Hol grabs my arm to be steady. I move her over to the side of the road, where she can walk in snow. Lake Street runs along the sea and is paved. They should call it Sea Street.

People who have a lot of money, or inheritance, or both, have their summer cottages on this street. But now the street is ours again, for another six months, and we take the "cut-through" past one of the cottages down to the sea.

Holly has chattered through much of this walk. It is her chance to speak with an adult. She relishes it. As for me, I have the problem that most men have, and many people. I don't listen well, but I try. Still, her voice blends in with the voices all around me. That of the chickadees, and nuthatches, and squirrels, and of course the pines. 'Tis true, the trees and rocks and stones themselves sing. There is Great Presence all around us, and I simply try to feel it.

We head up the beach. It is perfect for walking. The sand is frozen. The wind and sand and water breath kept the snow off the beach for a few yards. It is a dirty blond brown ribbon of God highway that separates the land and the sea.

Looking down it, I seem to see into infinity, the vanishing point. One side is tall cliffs, sometimes coated with pine and poplar and birch and cedar, and I am sure many wild creatures. Their tracks show up frozen into the beach at spots. Fossil-like tracks in the sand.

Sometimes the land side is too steep to support much, except sheer walls of clay and rock, sea oats, and scrub. These are the spots the children really like to climb, I tell Holly.

She doesn't comment.

All the voices have gotten her attention. We walk for miles up the beach just listening to the voices of the trees, of the sea.

Deep Saturday Morning Peace, on the shore of the sea. Just she and me.

It is snowing more heavily.

The islands offshore are no longer visible.

We proceed down to "one more point" and turn back.

At the "cut-through", we separate. I kiss her. Not a peck. A kiss. Between lovers. I begin to walk away but she calls me back, for a hug.

So we hug in silence, by the sea, in the Presence, in the deep silence, so full of voices, but none of them human, and perhaps, not audible to many humans. But only because they haven't tried.

I sigh.

We back away from each other and smile. And I turn and continue to walk down the beach, towards the harbor and town, to pick up a few things at the Mercantile.

This is the point when you, my friends and family, enter my head. All of you. I speak to you. In the present tense.

Let's lower our heads.

Let's walk the last half mile in peace. Feel the snow now settling heavily. Admire the great cedars and the white pines and a Christmas decoration here and there. Most of all, feel that Great Presence. It's everywhere. Settling. Cajoling. Wishing. Forgiving. Rejoicing. Blessing.

Up Sea—I mean Lake—Street. Cut through the woods this time. Down the rise. Past the house, to my office door.

I pause.

Shake the snow from my helmet hat. This morning Holly mentioned wanting to have it cleaned. Imagine that! Twelve years of good breaking in and she wants to clean it! Geesh! I told her, no, it would kill the head lice.

I brush the snow from my shoulders.

Step through the door.

I wish as you turn this page, that a little musical computer chip would come on playing...

"Angels we have heard on high..."

But since it can't, all I ask is that before you read what follows, go at least put this carol on, and then when it starts with.... " Angels we have heard on high...."

Begin to read.

Gabriel

Thanksgiving Day. The official kickoff to the celebration of the Coming. The first one.

It is still very black outside, early in the morning. The wind, the breath of everything, is roaring. Leaves clatter across the asphalt driveway. They pitter patter and clackle, as if someone, or something, is walking around outside my office door, pacing, or lurking. I'm not sure which.

We were unable to collect the leaves this year. The snows began early and stayed. Almost two feet we've had already. Two to four more inches are expected today. So the leaves are nestled in, under the white blanket of the winter's breath.

It was a few days ago.

What was a few days ago?

It was a few days ago that Mara and I took that walk.

What walk?

"That" walk.

Oh! **"That"** walk. Tell us about it!

Well....okay. If you insist.

The day began, much like this one. It was black as I sat and typed away in the early morning. The wind roared, fueled by the breath and energy of the North Pole, where I know it originated. If you stood out in it for more than a minute, and heard it rush through the pines, forcing them to speak the language of the winter pine, and blow against the bare oaks, black and vein-like, and heard it beat their branches, making them batter and crackle and pop, you would agree. This wind, from the North Pole, is a ferocious wind. Its power is immense, its magic deep. You should see what it does to the sea.

The day went fairly quickly. All days seem to go quickly now. Not just because the amount of daylight is down to about nine hours, they all just seem to race by.

Like time itself is in a hurry to get somewhere. Or maybe it's just in a hurry to be done. Until time is no more....

About four o'clock in the afternoon, which is really the beginning of our evening, Mara, my daughter, came sliding, and slithering into my office. This is not a snake slither. It is a Mara slither. How a nine-year old can be lanky and lithe and graceful all at once is beyond me. But Mara is.

Mara dances some sort of ballet through life. She doesn't walk, she moves here and there, always contemplating something in her environment, much of which can't be seen, at least not by me, or anyone else that I know of, except for maybe Noah, her twin brother.

Our twins, Mara and Noah, born of the same moment, are a tight duo, yet unbelievably different.

I wonder where Mara gets this stuff from.

"Dad?"

"What."

Notice, Mara's was a question. Mine was a statement. I was busy. Mara was bored.

"What are you doing?"

What this really means is..."What can you do with me?"

"Working, Mar."

I didn't add... "Isn't it obvious?"

There are times when I wonder if anything is obvious to Mara.

I sighed and twisted around on my secretarial swivel chair. I looked at her and smiled. She hung over the edge of the couch in my office in that typical Mara hanging lounge. Kind of like a leopard.

"What do you want to do, Mar?"

"Let's take a walk."

I sighed again and shrugged. It really didn't sound like a bad idea. Walking through the breath of the planet on such a fierce day would probably be a good idea. Refreshing.

Scintillating. A great departure from the mundane task of trying to earn a living. The key word there, may be "trying". Still.

Up I got, bones popping and cracking. Kind of like the giant oaks outside, I thought.

"We'd better dress warmly."

So we did.

Up the gentle rise in back of the house we trod. The snow really isn't that deep. Maybe a foot. It gets blown around a lot. And the sea is still arguing for control with the icy white blast of the Arctic. The sea breath is warm in comparison, even melting some of the very snow it makes.

The pines, hundred-foot sentinels of the backyard, rush and hush and sway. Pine talk. Snow swirls, sometimes getting caught up in whirlwinds that are like white tornadoes. These whipping dervishes are snow spirits. That's what the kids and I call them. You've all seen them before. Swirling snow caught up in a wind funnel anywhere from twenty to fifty feet high. We seem to have a lot of them here. They come and go and dance and blow. Some here are even a hundred feet high. They are particularly spectacular when they dance across the frozen surface of the sea. They move in no apparent order but yet are part of some Great Order. The Order of the Snow. We know, we belong to it.

I watch one that seems to be swirling around for a longer time than most. It's dancing next to a great white pine, of about ninety plus feet, about twenty feet away. It mesmerizes me. I glance at Mara for a second. She's staring at it, too.

"Mar, check out that snow spirit."

"Yeah." She says entranced.

The swirling spirit keeps twisting and revolving, but the air around it seems to settle, become different. Pushes out from it. Begins to dominate. Omnipresent. Pushing. Enveloping. No room for anything else. A smell. Where have I smelled that smell before? Sweet flowers. Overpoweringly sweet. Spring-like. Life scent. Grand, yet not suffocating.

In the middle of winter?!!!

What's going on here......

Wait a minute! I remember this smell. I've smelled it before! When that short, fat jolly little guy showed up a few years back, right after Halloween.....

Mara and I move over to the giant pine and hunker down beneath it. Perhaps we were seeking protection. Ten feet away the swirling snow spins and spins in a column now. Evening descends quickly. Amidst the snow clouds, deep sky, winter blue-black, envelopes. Light fades. A few stars twinkle and dance among the clouds and the stark tree branches. Still the column of swirling snow spins.

Something is happening to it.

Now there is a new sensation, or sense awakened.

Angels we have heard on high. Sweetly singing
o'er the plain. And the mountains in reply. Echo-
ing their glorious strains. Glorrrrrrrrr
rrrrrrrrrrr-or-i-a. In excelsis Deo......

From somewhere, something, or things, lots of things
were singing this song. It permeated the woods, the air, the
snow, everything. It's in everything, the trees, the ground,
the....

What's that?!!

What are those!??!!

Animals! Coming from all directions. Raccoons, too,
those masked bandits, waddling up towards the column.

I've got to tell you about these guys, the raccoons. I've
seen them before. One night I caught them on their nightly
stop at our garbage-dumpster-can-on-wheels. They were
wearing bandannas and sunglasses. There was a gang of
seven of them. And they were a gang. The only real gang

113

we have in this neighborhood. One would stand in front of the garbage can on all fours and the rest would use him as a step, right onto his back and into the can. The raccoon-proof latch proved little challenge. They'd all get in, munch out, throw a few scraps to Alfredo there on the outside, and smash all the trash down real well. Which is why I let this continue. They seldom left a mess outside the can and always mashed it down great. Natural compactors.

Anyway, here they were. Raccoons. This time with their little ones. Squirrels, too. All coming towards the column like it was the center of a great natural wheel, with them as spokes. Shrews, mice, Oh my! Deer! The prince of the forest, all twelve points of him, and his doe, and their fawns, no longer so little, now almost her size. Birds are now fluttering here and there, adding their own chorus to the singing. Everything is still singing. Cardinals, chickadees, Wow!

114

A huge red-headed pileated woodpecker. Every kind of animal seems to be coming.

> *Shepherds why this Jubilee? Why your joyous*
> *strains prolong?*

Oh my goodness!

Two large bears amble up and over the rise from the direction of the sea. One stands up and sniffs the air. Checking out the scene. They proceed towards the column. There is something in the column.

The sound is everywhere. It has all kinds of qualities. It seems to be in the air, yet in my head. It's deep, yet shrill, tingling, like chimes of all sorts.

> *What the gladsome tidings be? Which inspire your*
> *heavenly song? Glorrrrrrrrrrrrrrrrrrrrrrria!*
> *In excelsis Deo!*

Everyone gathers up towards the column now. Many of them are standing on their hind legs, those that have four.

They seem to be singing, too! They're all around us. We're in a sea of animals. Mara's got her mittened hand resting on the head of a ....fox!

I stand speechless, motionless, transfixed.

The singing slowly rises to the sky, softening, yet expanding, as if now in some Greater Power. It doesn't fade. It rises. Up. The stars become part of the song. One bright one in particular seems to hang over the tip of a blue spruce about thirty feet away. It's a beautiful Christmas-like spruce, about fifteen feet tall. Rays emanate from both the star and the tree. We all turn. The scene changes.

The air stops. So does time. Don't ask me how. It just does. And it is obvious.

Deep silence. Deep quiet.

We seem transported. A different continuum.

All eyes rest on the tree and the star, and now there is a woman. Barely. More like a just-teenaged girl. She's small, appears almost frail, yet hauntingly beautiful. She walks up to the tree, then turns to face the column, and smiles. The animals all walk over to her, surrounding her. They try to get as close as they can. She rests her slender, delicate, almost glowing hands upon their heads, and pets them. They sigh, collectively.

It seems as if she and the column are speaking.

I turn to look at the column.

Its brightness dazzles, like the sun reflecting off the water. The form inside now has a discernible shape. Boy-like, girl-like, Greek-mythology-like, young, old, new, ancient, but above all glorious, and very, very tall. Must be thirty feet.

I cannot describe their language. But it stirred my heart like nothing ever has before, and although I could never translate it, I seemed to know what they were talking about.

It seemed to be a memory.... a memory..... remembering

yet.... it was still alive! It was a living memory. No, more than a memory.

The girl and the form in the column laughed. And so did all the animals, indeed the winter trees and the pines shook with laughter. The world laughed.

They were recalling the moment, when It all began again.

The first time they'd met.

Which was still going on, two thousand years later.

A new awareness. Something far deeper than these heavenly creatures. Something incredibly overpowering was all around us. It frightened me, yet not horribly, just incredibly. It scared me. It suffocated me. It seemed like I was going to die!

The angel, yes, that's what it was! It was an angel in the column, although now it was the angel, no sign of any column. The angel and the woman-girl seemed to bow before It, and then they danced with It. No, not It! Him! It was

Him! Part of some sort of celebration. A never-ending celebration. The mother embraced Him. How did I know she was a mother?!!!

Perhaps The Mother.

The Mother who said, "Yes." The "yes" heard round the world. A tiny "yes", that began Life Itself, at the moment of conception, immaculate it is. Life begins at that moment. That "yes" is all the proof we'll ever need.

> "In His Image and Likeness He created them..." Genesis 1:26-27

How could there be a question of when life begins? Who are we to believe otherwise? Who are we to be otherwise?

Like a pebble dropped into the sea of all things and all times, the ripples from this "yes" grow outward and larger even to this day, rolling over the world, washing away the impurities.

"Behold, I am the handmaid of the Lord. May it be done to me according to your word." Luke 1:38

....Sweetly singing o'er the plain.

And God became Man.

"And the Word became flesh
and made His dwelling among us,
and we saw His glory,
the glory as of the Father's only Son,
full of grace and truth." John 1:14

Everything glowed. The animals, the woman-girl, the angel. The singing, now a great Gloria, glorious beyond all glory. Joy and Peace and Wonder abounded, like angels themselves, visible, touchable.

Smiles and laughter and great beauty!
Then the angel turned to me
And said....

"Remember"

Like someone had hit a huge gong, that "remember" entered into and saturated me. It caused me to vibrate, shake, sway. It struck me down and knocked me out.

When I woke, just Mara sat there, under the great white pine. She stared dreamily upwards, her hand still resting on the head of a small red fox, now curled up in a circle on her lap, eyes closed, its tail over the tip of its nose.

We sat there a long time. Mara and me and the fox.

The wind blew. Snow began to flit and flirt with the breathing wind and intensified. The stars disappeared. The tracks of all the animals were softly covered and whipped away.

At some point the fox got up, stretched, licked Mara's nose, and walked off into the deep gray and black and white night.

Mara and I stood up, stretched. We turned and walked

back down the rise. Our house nestled in the woods, lay before us. Candle lights, tiny beacons, starlike, stand in every window. A warm, cozy Christmas house. No doubt about it. We trudged through the snow towards it. The wind and the snow swirled and blew and made sparkles. Like deep, left-over magic from Somewhere far greater and far holier and far cozier.

"Dad?!"

"What, Mar?"

"Dad. You were talking to an angel."

A thousand times in my life, I would have answered her with…"I was?"

This time I simply said…

"I know."

"Dad."

"What, Mar?"

"I know who it was."

"I know you do, Mar. I know."

So did I.

Mara turned and looked at me and smiled. Then she turned back around and walked in front of me towards the house. I watched her for a few seconds before following. A little girl, soon to be a woman-girl, four years maybe separated her from the woman-girl of the pine tree, The Mother, from whence her name came.

The air still seemed full of song. Dancing song, stars hidden yet singing, snowflakes each a tiny chime of glory.

And the mountains in reply. Echoing their joyous strain.

On a deep and quiet night this Christmas season, go outside, if possible with a child, it doesn't have to be your own.

See if you can hear the singing.

It's everywhere.

For eternity.

And remember why we celebrate.
This day!
Called Christmas.
            Gloria!

LITTLE STAR

*N*ext to me, the printer runs the "final edition" of this year's Christmas letter, a record of a story. I will say no more about the story, except that a best friend named Tito asked in a September phone call from California that I say something in this year's letter about his brother-in-law and our good friend, Jeff.

In the middle of the night a few days later, my mind raced, and so the story you'll soon read.

Life on the Inside, up here, just a hair over half-way to the North Pole, inside the Leelanau Peninsula, is good. It is a cold and gray November day as I finish this story.

Christmas Unwrapped

There is a fire in the wood burner. The house is toasty. The kids constructed a fort outside from this year's load of fire wood, dumped earlier in the week, in the front yard. It calls me to come stack it, but the children's glee and imaginations prevent me from lifting a finger. Besides, without the fort, the bears, or something more fearsome, may get them.

It could be there in the Spring.

May the Stuff stars are made of shine on you, bring you Heaven-bred magic, and light up your Holidays with a gleam so bright it dispels your night and causes you to stare openmouthed, uttering the three-letter word that comes closest to describing the great Wonder of this Season...

"Wow!"

... And behold, the star that they had seen at its rising preceded them, until it came and stopped over the place where the Child was. They were overjoyed at seeing the star, and on entering the house they saw the Child with Mary, His mother...

Matthew 2:9-11

Little Star

In a time that is not of our time, in a space far, far away, there lived a little star.

Let go of your preconceived notions of time and space and transport yourselves to the universe of this little star, to the then time of stars and stars only. There you will meet Little Star, hear his story, and understand what he was and who he was and who he is.

Little Star was a real star. Very much like the ones you see in the heavens or the sky that lie above the planet on which we live. In the city you see only the brightest. Out in the country, where this story-teller lives, you can see all of them.

They are like a billion pinpricks of varying sizes, none ever being too bright, in a thick blanket that covers the night sky. Perhaps this is the best way to describe them. Think of

Someone taking a pin and poking holes for all eternity through a big thick black blanket. Unbeknownst to us on this the dark side of the blanket, on the other side is a Great Light. It is only through the pinpricks that you get to glimpse the Great Light.

So Little Star was one of these.

A pinprick.

Much like you and I are pinpricks in the great sea of humanity and the sands of time.

In those days of the Stars, the stars themselves were not unlike you and me and the rest of humanity. There were stars of different shapes and colors. There were stars of different brightnesses. There were some stars that dominated. There were some stars that were, oh so tiny, and almost insignificant.

Some stars radiated goodness. Some stars radiated, but not all of it was good. Stars would come and go. Sometimes even the same star would be brighter than at other times. Stars would dim. Stars moved around a lot, never stationary like they are today. Although, even today they are not stationary. They move. Now though, they move in a Great Order, as those that study them know. To you and me, the folk that just occasionally look up, they look still.

Stars in this then time of the stars and stars only behaved as individuals, interacting with each other and moving about at will. They worked together at times, such as star work is, creating nuclear fusion or fission.

Stars played together. They did good things for each other. Sometimes they did not-so-nice things to each other. These not-so-nice things could be catastrophic. To any of us within a hundred million light years of one of their not-so-nice pranks, it would be fatal.

The Stars of the then time of the stars and stars only depended on one another. In a sense, they lived off each other's energies. Stars came together to make other stars. A star attracted to another star would cause a reaction.

Star love. Think back to a time when you fell in love. This could be the first time. Or the time when you fell in love for good with one person. Or sometime in between. Or all of these. The key element I am trying to describe here is how you felt in the pit of your stomach. Let's call it love butterflies. That churning, I'll-never-sleep-again-oh-God-am-I-going-to-live-through-this-I'm-so-excited! feeling. The only thing that soothed you was to be in the presence of the person with whom you had "fallen in love". Even that didn't always work. It just replaced the anxiety of separation with the intensity of Presence. Most of us know what that intensity is like. The touch. The touch of a woman's hand upon the face of a man. The touch of a man's hand upon the face and then perhaps the neck of a woman. It goes from there.

Sparks fly.

So it was not much different with the Stars of the then time of stars and stars only. Two stars would meet, get to know one another, eventually sparks could or would fly. Hence, more stars. All stars came to be in this way.

Little Star was a "younger star" in a family of stars (for stars have families, too) from what we call the Pleiades system. All stars have names. Today you may know them as Sirius, or Alpha Centauri, or Omega 34A. This was the same in the then time of stars and stars only.

Little Star's name was Joseph. But from almost day one of Little Star's existence everyone called him Little Star.

Perhaps this was because Little Star had an older brother of a star who was much bigger, much brighter, and very popular among all the other stars.

You might expect to see a little jealousy seep into the story at this point. Here's Big Brother, a big-guy-on-campus who hangs out with a lot of sensational beauty stars, very popular, very cool. Little brother comes to the same campus and you would expect the light of the big brother to shine too bright and put the light of the little brother in some sort of shadow, eventually causing a rift, an estrangement of a family relationship.

Not in the case of Little Star. Little Star was so amiable, so unassuming, and so proud of Big Brother Star that he was happy just to be around him. To the credit of Big Brother Star, he always watched out for Little Star, never lording it over him, keeping a good eye on him, and smiling at him a lot.

Actually, most stars smiled a lot at Little Star. He was one of those rare stars who was just a good star. He always tried to do his best, made himself agreeable to other stars, and had no extraordinary star gifts that might cause him to become too powerful, or too greedy, or too ambitious. He was simply a good star. In our terminology, we would say...

"He's a good guy!"

... and really mean it.

In the then time of stars and stars only such an accolade was rare. Just as it is for us today. Look at all the people you know. Read the paper for a week. Watch the news for two nights. Then tell me how many people there are who are virtuous but don't boast, who never get under your skin, and who, when you think about them, you think nothing bad, indeed only good. Yet, they haven't done anything stellar. I mean they are a good husband and father, or wife and mother, or even a good kid. Still, their actions do not set the world on fire or give them any significant recognition. They just quietly go about being the best they can, doing all they can for those around them, rarely being recognized. Yet, everyone wants to call them friend.

Such was Little Star.

The "world" or universe of the stars of the then time of stars and stars only was a mean and chaotic place. Many stars wanted more than they deserved and often took it at the expense of other stars, sometimes even causing the light in the stars they took from to go out, or be severely dimmed.

Look around our world. See the pain, the agony, people cause other people in their quest for power or out of greed or ostensibly in the name of religion or for survival. Look at the bodies. See their life's red essence, tainted chocolate syrup brown, spilled on a sidewalk. Know that their friends and relatives will never talk to them again on this earth. See the people who starve, their stomachs bloated from lack of nourishment. Worse yet, see their children.

Stop for a moment and picture these things. It is difficult, I know. It will cause you to be squeamish and perhaps put down this paper, not wanting to read anymore. Well, right now I don't want you to read anymore. I want you to immerse yourself in the agony of the world. Be with the child who just turned thirteen and is lying in trash on a cold step in New York City with insects crawling through her soiled, ragged clothes. She is pregnant, dying of AIDS, and wanting desperately a Mom, or Dad, and having neither.

So the universe of the then time of stars and stars only was not much different. The stars fought. They gouged. The only real difference is that the effect of the stars upon the stars was truly stellar in scope. Think of two people colliding. Now put that in the terms of stars. The impact was far greater. Indeed the fate of the entire Universe could be said to be at stake.

But, in the middle of all this chaos and meanness and selfishness shone Little Star.

Everybody loved him. One star in particular.

Her name was Tinuviel, a name given her by the Maker of all stars, the Great One, meaning "the daughter of twilight". You may read the name of Tinuviel in many other stories. J.R.R. Tolkien describes Tinuviel as an elf. Could be, but this Tinuviel was a star. Maybe this star was the first Tinuviel.

And when Tinuviel and Little Star got together—sparks flew.

Stars didn't marry, at least not in the sense we do. Often they would come together, and if they were of opposing genders, he versus she stars, sparks would fly. Sometimes little stars would come to be, sometimes not. Often these stars would stay together in the star sense.

They could not be physically together all the time; the nuclear reaction would short out the universe. But they could commit to each other.

Some stars committed for their entire lives, as the laws of the universe demanded. Some remained committed to each other for awhile and then drifted off, perhaps becoming tired of their partner's color, or brightness, or losing their partner to a star whose color, or brightness, appealed more.

Joseph, Little Star, loved Tinuviel very much. Tinuviel loved him very much. In the selfishness of the universe of the then time of stars and stars only, their love created an oasis of kindness. Love radiated from them like the light that it was, star clean, star bright, first light of the night.

One day one spark stuck. Little Star and Tinuviel had a little star. Two became three.

In the preceding paragraph consisting of three simple sentences perhaps we can get a glimpse, just a tiny glimpse, of the meaning of Trinity. We celebrate Christmas because of the birth of the Son of God. The Father, Who gave us the Son, Who left us the Spirit. Two are Three are One. So in the great Thread of all creation we see a connection.

Little Star, Tinuviel, and Child Star, as the little star of Little Star and Tinuviel became known, were very merry happy and, in the middle of the great chaos of their universe, were doing well.

They stuck to the laws of the universe, especially Little Star, even when most stars didn't.

Despite all the corruption and ugliness made by the stars of the then time of stars and stars only, the Universe was still a beautiful place to be. Much like our Good Mother Earth, even though gouged by man, is still an artwork of Creation and a beautiful place to be!

As time passed, stars, simply because they liked him, began to give Little Star things to do. These tasks gave him more security and a higher position in the then time of stars and stars only. He was moving up in the universe. Everyone was happy, especially Tinuviel and Child Star.

Often the new tasks that Little Star had to do to maintain the status he had attained and to continue the work of creation to which he was assigned meant he had to travel.

He went and worked with other stars in different places of the then universe, often commuting to different galaxies. Travel then, like now, is not without its perils.

Perils.

Men and women used to put to sea. For months at a time they would leave their loved ones. Standing there on the shore as the boat departed these loved ones would wonder if they would ever see their spouses again. Many times they did not.

Today, people still "put to sea", but for much shorter times. They take cars, trains, and planes. Tragedy still strikes, but not nearly as often as it used to. We accept that travel and its perils are part of people's jobs in the great work of Creation. As always, still it goes on. Life.

The perils of travel during the then time of stars and stars only were great. Many things could happen to a star traveling about the Universe. Cosmic winds could blow a star way off course, or into collision with another star, much like two cars crashing. The power and greed of other stars, or systems of stars, often caused problems. Gravitational fields would become too powerful and stars would be sucked into a system never to escape, or would be extinguished altogether. There were stars that lurked about preying on traveling stars, seeking to take all, or part, of another star's life essence, their nuclear energy for their own use, caring little if it caused death. Stars often chose to travel together for safety. Much like we have done throughout our history and even today. People take planes because it is faster, and statistically it is safer to travel in a plane, together, than in a car.

Sometimes the unintentional carelessness of a single star, or the application of some universal force beyond the control and force of the stars, would cause a group of traveling stars to suddenly career wildly out of control. These disasters were unimaginable in their destructiveness. Like comparing a plane crash to a car crash.

The result of such a collision was the stars' worst nightmare...

A black hole.

With a black hole, nothing is left. No light. No sound. No smell. Not even a whiff of cosmic dust. Just emptiness and eternal blackness. Nothing escapes and anything that gets too close is sucked in forever.

It was in the ninth phase of that parsec of the then time of stars and only stars... (Stars didn't keep track of the hours, days, months, or number of parsecs. Stars of the then time of stars and stars only had no use for the concept of time. They just knew there were twelve phases that repeated themselves over and over)..... As I say, it was in the ninth phase that the greatest tragedy known to stars of the then time of stars and stars only struck the family of Little Star.

On one of his trips to secure things for Tinuviel and Child Star and to continue the work of Creation, Little Star and the group of stars with whom he was traveling were involved in a cosmic collision and were sucked into a black hole.

The then universe noticed when this great tragedy happened. You might miss a car crash in the news, but you never miss a plane crash.

Tinuviel knew instantly, even before the other stars spread the news like starfire.

Her light dimmed, indeed it almost went out. If it hadn't been for the need to care for Child Star, it might well have burnt out.

The black hole might as well as been inside of her, at least where her heart used to be.

Tinuviel told Child Star. He took it well. Much better than any of the other stars. Maybe it was because he was too young to know any better. Maybe it was because he was wise beyond his parsecs. All the friends of Little Star were filled with grief. Star tears flooded the sky as meteors and comets. Thousands gathered at the edge of the black hole.

Before long the stars began, one by one, to talk about Little Star. They praised him, they glorified him, they took solace in the friendship with each other—all because of Little Star.

Finally, Child Star, all on his own, got up above the host of stars and told what it was like to be the son of Little Star and how great a star dad Little Star was. There wasn't a dim star in the gathering spot. Meteors and comets covered the heavens like a spring cloudburst, drenching the black skies. The universe filled with these tears of the stars. So much so, that as parsecs went by, even stars that had never known Little Star came to ask what the heavenly display was all about.

Eventually, the stars went back to their places in the

universe. The emptiness never really left any of them, but most of all it never left Tinuviel.

Yet, she went on. As stars do.

Some parsecs later, Tinuviel became concerned about Child Star. Child Star seemed to be spending a lot of time in the area where Little Star had been sucked into the black hole. Hovering dangerously close to the edges.

Usually, Child Star was never a problem. In fact, he seemed to be created in the image and likeness of his father. He was just as wonderful, just as kind, a true joy for any star mother.

But that hovering around the black hole. It worried Tinuviel and reminded her constantly of the death of Little Star.

One day, in the twelfth phase of that stellar year, something happened that was to signal the change of the universe of the then time of stars and stars only, forever.

145

Child Star came back from the black hole one day and said...

"There's something in the black hole where Star Father disappeared, Star Mother. I can see it. It's like a tiny pinprick of light! It even looks like it might be starlight!"

He said this with such quiet excitement and firm belief that Tinuviel's star heart almost stopped. Her light fluttered. Darkened for a moment. Then came back with a spit of light that could only be described as hope, yet darkened again as quickly as it had appeared bright.

Stars of the then time of stars and stars only had no future and no past, they lived in a time in which everything always was. History was life, and so all stars knew all the absolutes of what had ever happened as well as the laws of the universe.

So, Tinuviel said..

"That is impossible, Child Star. You must have been seeing things. Nothing could ever exist inside a black hole. It is the end of existence."

"But I saw something, Mother!"

Determinedly, Child Star kept watch around the edge of the black hole into which Little Star had disappeared. It was about a dozen phases later when he again came streaking across the galactic sky and screeched up in comet-like fashion to report to his star mother...

"The Light is back. And it's brighter!"

Tinuviel looked at Child Star, ready again to remind him of the laws of the universe and the knowledge of history that was star life, when she stopped. In the center of Child Star she saw a quiet brightness. A pure light. It reminded her of something. Perhaps Little Star? Or something else? Or something more!?

She sighed.

"Let me come look with you."

They arrived at the edge of the black hole and hovered, struggling to keep from being sucked in by its black pull. Child Star was quiet for a long time before he said...

"Look, there it is!"

Tinuviel strained, but could see nothing. For a long time they hovered. Tinuviel never saw anything but the great blackness.....

Life went on. Child Star became more and more like Little Star. Stars often commented and smiled at his likeness to Little Star.

The only thing that caused them to wonder about Child Star was that every twelfth phase he went back to hover around the black hole where Little Star had disappeared.

"Unhealthy!" they exclaimed.

"Weird!" said others.

"Oh no!" said Tinuviel.

One day, a friend of Child Star's decided to sneak out and

spy on Child Star as he made his annual journey in the twelfth and last phase of the stellar light year to the edge of the black hole.

This star's name was John.

Over the edge of Child Star's corona peeked John into the depths of the inner blackness.

Suddenly he saw... a pinprick of light!

He gasped!

Child Star spun around immediately and peered at first in fright, then in sudden scrutiny, wise beyond his parsecs, into the center of John.

"You see it, too!"

Child Star said this with such conviction that he could not be denied. John admitted seeing the impossible—a pinprick of light in the center of the black hole.

At first only the younger stars came. All of them could see the pinprick now becoming a pinpoint. Eventually the older stars' curiosity overcame them and they too began to come. Most of the older stars couldn't see anything. Then a few began to.

This caused the Word to spread like starfire! And the belief!

It was on a day late in the twelfth phase, of what was to become known as the very last phase of the then time of stars and stars only, that Tinuviel returned to the black hole.

A great throng of stars had gathered, sensing something was going to happen that never happened before. All the stars parted before Tinuviel.

Tinuviel coasted to the edge of the black hole, the most feared place in all of stardom. She pulled up next to and touched the corona of Child Star. Then she shifted her gaze from the center of her son's light to the center of the black hole.

It was there she saw the Light.

She recognized it immediately.

It was Little Star's.

Tinuviel burst into a flood of star tears, meteors and comets. Her tears of recognition enabled all the other stars to see the pinpoint of Light. Then they began to recognize in this Light the light of all the other stars who had gone before them into black holes, or otherwise suffered the extinguishment of their lights.

The pinpoint began to move. Outwards!

It began to grow in size, becoming larger and brighter! The stars realized that the pinpoint was not a pinpoint but an opening, an opening to a Place beyond the black blanket of the night sky heavens.

And this opening of Light came from the very center of a star's greatest fear, a star's worse death, the dreaded Black Hole.

All chaos ceased. All selfishness died in a great shrill

shriek. All evil became undone in the Great Light. All black holes ceased to be.

The stars, led by Child Star, entered into the Light.

The joy was overwhelming! The celebration a masterpiece of all existence! The most phenomenal party ever! Reunited were the stars with what they thought was forever lost.

As they entered the Place, they joined in a dance of supreme merriment and happiness. A dance of the Greatest Order. All the stars fell willingly and happily into this grand dance of celebration, leaving in the now gone universe behind them the then time of stars and stars only.

In the center of the dancing stars stood a single Great Star. The Orchestrater of the celebration.

As the stars reached the point of greatest satisfaction, of complete reunion with lost ones, of overwhelming peace, this Great Star asked them to follow Him.

The heavens moved. In perfect procession. Gone were all the problems and chaos, the deaths, the greeds, the powers. All became One in the Great Order of the sky we know today.

The entire host came to rest in a spot of what is now our known universe. They hovered above a tiny, insignificant planet, green and blue and brown and troubled.

The Great Star turned to Little Star and said.....

"It is time."

Little Star turned to Child Star and said....

"This task is appointed to you. Because you are from me, as I am from the star fathers before me, and have remained true to all that is good, and because I was good, but mostly because **you chose to believe**, this is your hour. May all the stars, especially the Great Star, shine in you, through you, at this appointed hour of the **change of all things.**"

Child Star began to decrease a little in size, more, then a

little more. The entire host of stars watched in wonder and fascination. How could a star do such a thing and live? As it became clear this Star was alive and going to stay that way, the decreasing caused great excitement. Eventually Child Star became small enough that he could rest comfortably over the small planet. He emanated a bright light, one that anyone who lived on the planet would recognize as being something completely out of the ordinary. From the light's center came a beam.

No one in the Heavens could mistake this beam.

It was the beam of the Stuff of which stars are made, and all else. From the Great One, Himself, the Maker of all stars.

The beam shone forth from the center of Child Star in a brilliant shaft, shining intently onto that one small planet, onto one small town, onto the very Source of What was, What is, What will be…a tiny baby. A tiny baby who would eventually walk among the people of that planet so that they, too, could know the Place behind the black blanket and the Source of The Great Light, and be One with the stars and each other and Him, for eternity.

The stars have since held their place in the great celebration that began that day one thousand nine hundred and ninety four of our years ago. They are in perpetual adoration around the Great Star. The phases have ceased and become months.

We have years now all marked by our passing around the star given to us in the very beginning by the Great Star, since the day He came, the day when Child Star gave us the sign that He was here.

The trials and tribulations of the then time of the stars and stars only have passed to us, along with the selfishness, evil, and the great tragedies.

But every so often there comes along a Little Star to show us and other child stars the way when we become lost.

Even if the way is through a black hole and out into the Other Side and be it years before we can follow.

On one of the great star-filled nights that manifest themselves here on our planet in unearthly splendor, I took a walk with a then seven-year old.

My son, Noah.

Noah is a tad afraid of the dark. The path through the forest up to the top of the hill, where we go to see the stars better, can be a bit intimidating in the dark for a seven-year old. Trees become great giants with a hundred arms each and a dozen claws on the end of each arm. But with the help of my hand and the reminder of the reality of his guardian angel, he always makes it through, past the dark spirits and into the clearing where we can peek up at, and into, the heavens.

We gazed in quiet wonder that night. Wowed at a couple of shooting stars. Basked in the heavenly light.

Noah spoke quietly.

"You know what Dad."

"What Noah."

"I think the brightest star, that Great Star right up there, is Jesus. And all the other stars are people that have gone to heaven and are up there celebrating. Boy, are they celebrating! It's better than any fireworks!"

The One did come down late in the twelfth phase, on the twenty-fifth day, and opened the door to these heavens. One of His heavenly creations, a star, small by universal standards, but great to the eyes that beheld its miraculous light, announced to all who would look up, the event of all history.

Though a man-designated day forces a once-a-year memory, we are constantly reminded by the stars themselves and by little children.

My children often ask which one is Child Star, the Christmas Star. It has become difficult for any of us to see.

When you look up into the heavens this Christmas, try and see it.

Remember all those who have gone before us.

If you believe, you will see.

And don't forget to celebrate!

Christmas Unwrapped

I wrote this story for Eileen (Tedaldi) O'Keefe and her son Ryan, at the request of her brother Rick, whom we call Tito. It is in loving memory of her husband, Jeff, and Ryan's father, our friend whom we nicknamed in college, Little Star. Jeff died in the USAir plane crash of September, 1994, that went down in Pittsburgh. Pittsburgh was his home.

This story is theirs. For I am just a simple star gazer, and have merely told what I have seen. Please keep them in your prayers always, but especially at this most Holy time of year, and one where they will sorely miss their Little Star, a black hole to be endured, until that Time when there will be no more time and no more tragedies.

> *Encourage the children of this world to show greater care and solicitude for the things of eternity than for those of time.* St. Ignatius

Letter Seven
THE LAST CHRISTMAS

*Y*ears of thinking and wondering and writing about Christmas passes like a star dropping from the sky. I blink, and sit, trying to put into readable shape these mental wanderings.

I wonder if I'll ever write of Christmas again...

I probably will.

I hope so.

After all, isn't that a big part of Christmas, too?

Hope!

This past Christmas, and the last one of this book, is over by a full phase of the moon. The next celebration is now under eleven cycles of our Great Sister Moon away.

Before I began to jot down these final thoughts, I stood outside this morning, in single digit air, and watched the Moon, Venus, and Jupiter position themselves for a perfect line dance, across the Eastern sky. They were beautiful. They pranced to the song of the wind, made perfect by the whistling of its great breath through the towering sentinels of ever dark green, our huge white pines. Whishing, swooshing, speaking through the pines' needles, blowing away the imperfections of men and women, settling down to the quiet perfection of God.

Now it is time to finish this recording. The work, the drudgery of editing begins. Years and countless hours of typing and dreaming and hoping you will read this and be touched, not by me but by the Spirit who lives through me, and Who allows me to live, now come to the point of purifi-cation. Will I be able to help you believe?

So what about this last Christmas?

Our traditional remembrance was challenged this past year. It is impossible to put into words the pain of physical health impairment, the failure of our dwelling to do its job, the consequent doctor bills and repair bills, the quagmire of debt unplanned, and the uncertainty of how to pay for it. These things happened to us, and then as Christmas ap-proached, we were unable to even decorate as we normally do.

But we did our best.

There were fewer lights, fewer votive candles, fewer Christmas carols, fewer presents to give. Even the weather refused to cooperate. Christmas morning woke to green grass, the first in thirteen years and the second in fifty, here on the Inside, where we live.

The children began to question the reality of Santa Claus, or St. Nicholas, his rightful name. Ten- and eight- and eight-years old these children. The oldest and the twins.

They wanted to know for sure that He was real. No tricks now Dad, no fooling, swear you are telling the truth.

The tooth fairy had fallen two months before Christmas. Our oldest, Logan, had lost a tooth, and without a word, put it under his pillow. He forsook the traditional pouch that Mom keeps for just such an occasion. The tooth fairy pouch we have all used.

So Mom didn't know a tooth was out and waiting under the pillow of a ten-year old boy to be claimed by that magical person, the tooth fairy. That following morning, as Mom woke him for school, he immediately went for the spot under the pillow, and instead of finding a dollar, he found his tooth.

Expressing disappointment to his mother, she quickly countered with, "You didn't use the pouch."

163

This explanation lasted for only a few minutes as the oldest came down the steps with...

"There really isn't a tooth fairy, is there, Mom?"

Not wanting to deal with this reality Mom said...

"Don't wreck it for your brother and sister. We can't talk about this now, we'll talk about it after school."

He didn't waste a moment after school. He wanted to talk and to know. Now.

So his mother told him.

I wouldn't have. I would have figured out some metaphysical explanation that blended reality with Reality. But she just told him.

He broke down and cried. So did she.

He expressed shock that we had lied to him.

Ooooo!

Touché!

As he left the room, he turned, and looking at his mother

with tear-stained cheeks with still very much a little boy's face....

He said....

"Mom, thank God there is still Santa!"

Christmas came, and so did Santa. Despite the chaos of repair to our home it was a good celebration. Despite the lack of funds, the three children received what they asked for, much to their delight. Some of this satisfaction is due to the fact they don't ask for much.

No TV for eighteen months reduces the exposure to materialism that sucks away at the values of society and places the emphasis on what you have, versus what you do or who you are.

There was a lot of conversation about Santa prior to Christmas. The three still wrote notes, to be picked up by St. Nicholas on his feast day, December 6th. He still came and got the notes. And left treats in their stockings in place of the notes. No coal, no sticks, just tangerines and sweets. These are good children. They are a tribute to their mother.

The notes had a few gift requests, and they also had something else. These notes to Santa, St. Nicholas, had pictures of the note writers and little sentences that while short, and childlike, said more than this, or any book, could ever say.

They said...."Santa, I still believe in you and I love you."

The curiosity over Santa didn't let up. Several times I was asked if he was real. I replied with the truth. Yes, he is real. Prepared to define this, I was never asked. But they began to speculate, and the first understanding of the Spirit world, which I believe is the Real world, the never-ending one, came into the mind of these three.

This world, the one that holds this page, and this print, and the things you see as you look up right now from this page, is only the shadow of reality, or as C.S. Lewis describes it—the Shadowlands.

Sometime this year we will talk about the Spirit of Santa Claus and good St. Nick. I will teach them how Real they really are.

After church services on Christmas Eve, we opened one present each, ate lots of good stuff: clams, shrimp, cookies.

About ten in the evening the children and I decided to go for a Christmas Eve walk. Poking around for coats and gloves and hats, the temperature having dipped into the twenties, we talked about Christmas Eve, and Christmas, and the magic. You know, The Magic.

"Christmas Eve is the most magical night of the year!" exclaimed Mara to her two brothers. Her smile, her tone, her glee said much more than the words.

There was no argument from the other two. Just bursts of agreement. The excitement was contagious. I could feel it. Smell it. Almost become it. The excitement of a little child on Christmas Eve. Pure.

We stepped outside.

The heavens were filled with stars. Where we live there are few houses, none within immediate view of our home (home mind you, not house), and cars seldom pass. It was just us, the pines, the great now-bare oaks and maples, and the stars.

We followed our normal walking path that takes us down to the sea. It was but a few minutes when things began to happen. Before I tell you what they were, I want to take you to the end of the walk. This is a writer's prerogative, to change the order of things.

As we chugged down the lane that leads us back to our home, greatly excited now about what had just happened (Don't worry, you'll find out), there appeared in the eastern sky..... Something.

To this day, we have never been able to confirm what it was. Let me try and describe it, my version, the kids' version, and Holly's version. Logan and Mara ran about two hundred yards to the house to get Mom and drag her out and up the hill to where we were. She was already in her pajamas, but I had to get "adult" confirmation.

Hanging just above the trees, was a...

Light? Star? Oscillation? Aberration? UFO?

Like a bright spotlight, this thing hung, no, it hovered over the trees in the eastern horizon. I thought at first it might be Sirius, it being the brightest star in the heavens, playing tricks with our eyes. But no, wrong time of year, wrong place in the sky.

It was a very bright star-like light that had an oscillating pulse to it, showing twinges of red and green.

One of us thought it was a UFO, the twins were sure it had something to do with Santa, and I, I just wondered if it was the star, you know, The Star, The Christmas Star.

For many moments we watched this great light in the

heavens dance about over the tree tops. It never revealed to us what it really was.

We've never seen it since that magical night.

The best of all though, was earlier. Yes, back to the part of this letter where I took you to the end.

I think Noah was the first to spot Him.

Streaking across the Christmas Eve sky. Santa. So fast you could barely focus.

It wasn't long before Mara and Logan saw Him, too. They shouted with glee and confirmation.

"Nah! No way!" - I can hear you all saying this to yourselves right now. Doubts leaping at me across the currents of time and distance.

Well, I'm telling you, cross my heart and hope to die and go ahead and stick a needle in my eye, they saw him!

Yeah, really! Santa! In the sky! Ask any of my kids, they'll tell you. He was there.

There are people that would have tried to convince these children that they were seeing "things", meteors, perhaps.

I didn't say a word.

I didn't even look up.

I didn't need to.

You see, I know He was there.

He came just to prove to my kids again, one more time, maybe even the last time for them for a long, long time, maybe until they have children of their own, that He was real.

I believe. And so do they.

I should know, I taught them.

Imagination is more important than knowledge.

Albert Einstein

Maybe you should take a walk next Christmas Eve. Late. Make sure you take a child. They can see much better.

And keep your eyes peeled!

Licking The Envelope

*T*he final act of any letter is to lick the envelop and seal it. After that, the letter ceases to be yours and becomes the person's to whom you send the letter.

Now all these letters are yours.

A very old friend of many of us came hustling into my head as the finishing touches were put on this book.

He looked as scary as the last time I saw him.

His face shown as the sun. His hair and beard long and snow-white flowed out from his head as if blown back by the winds of eternity.

He held a staff that might be platinum.

His robes showed all the shades of gold one could ever imagine.

His smile dazzled me, teeth of star light.

I think he wanted to make, or maybe remake, a point. Besides, I sense he wanted this group of letters to have a fitting conclusion.

He spoke…..

> *However, take care and be earnestly on your guard not to forget the things which your own eyes have seen, nor let them slip from your memory as long as you live, but teach them to your children and to your children's children.* Moses

He said these words once before, oh so very long ago.

Before the birth of the Master, after speaking with The Master's Father.

You can find them in Deuteronomy Chapter 4, Verse 9.

ADDITIONAL INFORMATION

Consider giving a copy of *Christmas Unwrapped* to
someone special. It's a perfect stocking stuffer or
a mystical way to say "I love you."

For only $12.95 (plus $3.50 shipping and handling), add
warmth to someone's Christmas.
Order your copies today!

Rhodes & Easton
121 E. Front St., 4th Floor
Traverse City, MI 49684
1-800-706-4636
616-933-0448 (fax)

CHRISTMAS UNWRAPPED

Cover design by Eric Norton

Text design by Mary Jo Zazueta
in Bell MT

Text stock is 55 lb. Writers Natural

Printed and bound by McNaughton & Gunn
Saline, Michigan

Production Editor: Alex Moore